The Christmas Virtues

The
CHRISTMAS
VIRTUES

A Treasury of Conservative Tales
for the Holidays

EDITED BY

JONATHAN
V. LAST

TEMPLETON PRESS

Templeton Press
300 Conshohocken State Road, Suite 500
West Conshohocken, PA 19428
www.templetonpress.org

Designed and typeset by Gopa & Ted 2, Inc.

Library of Congress Cataloging-in-Publication Data on file.

Printed in the United States of America

15 16 17 18 19   10 9 8 7 6 5 4 3 2 1

For Cordelia Mary, my princess

Contents

Acknowledgments

So here we all are. Third time's the charm.

Every writer secretly wants to do a trilogy at some point in his career, and after *The Seven Deadly Virtues* and *The Dadly Virtues*, this book was almost called *Revenge of the Virtues*. But Susan Arellano had a better idea.

I owe large debts to two women for this book, and the first is to Susan, the mastermind of Templeton Press. She was a good friend before we published this series and is now pretty much family. And not only that, but the entire idea for *The Christmas Virtues* was hers. There's no trilogy without Susan. And not just her, but her entire team at Templeton Press, especially Trish Vergilio, who produced this book on an impossible schedule, Tomás Puyans and Angelina Horst, who did a million little things to smooth the way, and Bob Land, who has copyedited the entire series with care and precision.

And of course, there wouldn't be a Templeton Press without the wonderful support of the John Templeton Foundation and Sir John Templeton, Dr. Jack Templeton, and Heather Templeton Dill. My deep thanks to them as well.

Thanks also to my dear friend Adam Keiper, of the *New Atlantis*, who stepped in to help me with my introduction at a difficult moment. And to my bosses at the *Weekly Standard*, Bill Kristol and Fred Barnes—not only for taking me in as a wayward youth and making my adult life possible—but for putting together a magazine full of brilliant writers I could conscript.

It was great fun rounding up the gang for one last mission. If you read either *The Dadly Virtues* or *The Seven Deadly Virtues*, you'll know almost everyone in this book: Rob Long, James Lileks, P. J. O'Rourke, Christopher Buckley, Andrew Ferguson, Christopher Caldwell, Matt Labash, Stephen Hayes, Jonah Goldberg, Mollie Hemingway, David Burge, Joe Queenan, Sonny Bunch, Larry Miller, Michael Graham, Joseph Epstein, and Toby Young are all old friends by now. I'm grateful to them for coming along on this adventure.

But we did add two new writers this time around: Kirsten Powers and Heather Wilhelm. I've admired them both for years and am privileged to have them on the team and count them as friends now, too.

The other big debt is due to my dear wife, Shannon. I always say that she's my editor of first and last resort, but it's true. She's one of the most gifted editors (and writers) I know. Her fingerprints are all over this book, though you'd never know it, because she's that good. Unless you're a writer, you can't imagine what a comfort it is to have so much talent sleeping next to you every night. And in addition to everything else, she is my love.

Cody John Paul (age seven) and Emma Elisabeth (age two) were not quite as helpful, though they each did their bit. It was Cody who revealed to me the deep ontological truths of Christmas on the day, just after Easter, that he came into the world. And Emma, who narrowly avoided being born on December 25th, was the best Christmas present I'll ever get.

My final thanks goes to Cordelia Mary, who is five, and to whom this book is dedicated. Like Britain and the United States, Cordelia and I have always had a special relationship. An example: A year ago or so, she and I had a rare moment of conflict, at the conclusion of which she shouted, "My heart is *mad* at you."

In a not-perfect moment of parenting, I retorted, "My heart is mad at you, too."

Cordelia stared at me, blue eyes blazing. And then she said, slowly, deliberately, and with stony finality, "Well, *your* mad heart still belongs to *me*."

It did. It does. And it always will. I love you, my Red. All the way.

—JVL

The Christmas Virtues

Introduction

The Miracle of Christmas

Jonathan V. Last

I WAS RAISED Catholic and educated by Quakers, but as a child, my real devotion was to the Church of Santa Claus.

At home, my Catholicism was mostly cultural, the kind of legacy birthright that came standard-issue for South Jersey kids in the 1980s. We went to church on Christmas and Easter and, occasionally, during ordinary time. The pope was a figure of distant admiration. When my grandfather was particularly agitated he would mutter "Jesus, Mary, and Joseph"—though always more in the spirit of perturbation than petition.

At school the Quakers believed, theoretically, in Christmas. They would put a tree up in the office, though in retrospect that may have been the doing of the school's chief administrator, an intensely Irish woman named Pauline Martin. And they hosted a craft bazaar every December where children were encouraged to buy presents for their families, though even my childhood self understood that this was more a fund-raising exercise than a celebration. But they did hold a Christmas pageant, once. I was in second grade, and I remember being slightly confused because it was the first time I'd ever heard Jesus, Mary, or Joseph mentioned by anyone from the Society of Friends. As far as the Quakers were concerned, the real Holy Trinity was composed of George Fox, Dag Hammarskjöld, and the United Nations.

For my own part, I believed in Santa. I diligently sent a letter every December—not a wish list, but more of a "How are you doing? Can't wait to see you!" I'd write him another on Christmas Eve, asking all sorts of questions and thanking him for stopping by. I'd leave it on the coffee table in the living room with milk and cookies, plus carrots for the reindeer. Then, on Christmas morning, I'd sneak downstairs before the clock ticked five.

The tree twinkled with tinsel and colored lights, presents spread beneath it like rolling foothills. But the first thing I'd do was check to see if Santa had written back. He had, always, and so I'd sit with his note, reading it over and over. Then I'd carry it with me as I crept quietly among the presents, appraising each one, but never disturbing their arrangement. I would take my stocking down, gently empty it, examine the little wonders, and carefully repack it. And then I'd sit on our ugly cream-colored sofa clutching the note while gazing at the presents and the tree for an hour in something like quiet contemplation.

These hours—there were probably seven of them, total— were the happiest of my childhood. I felt as though I held in my hand a kind of magic that belonged only to me, and between this miracle, the lights, and the stillness, I felt for the first time the beautiful calm of reverence. Toward Santa.

I believed in him profusely, profoundly, long past the age when my friends had torn away the shroud. And if really pressed, I'd tell you that I still believe, a little bit. When you are, as poker pros say, pot-committed to the idea of the Virgin Birth, then an eight-hundred-year-old saint who warps space-time in order to crisscross the globe scribbling notes and dispensing gifts seems fanciful, to be sure. Yet with God, all things are possible.

But this is not a book about Santa, even though David Burge (aka the Great and Powerful Iowahawk) has a blockbuster look at what really goes on at the North Pole. It's not about Christmas trees, or presents, or kids on Christmas morning, though

Christopher Caldwell, Heather Wilhelm, and Steve Hayes have wonderful chapters on those subjects, too.

The Christmas Virtues is actually an extended meditation on the idea that Christmas is not really for children. Children love Christmas, of course, but they can merely see the shiny surface of it. The true wonder of Christmas lies in mysteries so deep that only adults can appreciate them. Viewed properly, the holiday does not become dull and routine over the years; it becomes more startlingly, achingly majestic. To take just one example: Children cannot understand the ontological truth that creation is inherently an act of love.

Now don't worry—this isn't a book about ontology or philosophy or theology. It's about how we live Christmas. So actually, it *is* about trees and presents and Christmas morning—and a whole lot else.

If you're one of those people who likes to open presents on Christmas Eve—that's fine. No judgment. You can skip ahead to Rob Long's bizarrely compelling defense of Scrooge, which is just a few pages away. But before you go, I want to talk for just a moment about the creeping secularism that has become entangled with Christmas in America these days. Jonah Goldberg has a chapter about what my wife and I jokingly refer to as the GWoC. (That's the "Global War on Christmas" to you civilians.) I don't want to spoil it for you, but trust me, it's great.

This is not an actual war, of course. Lawsuits are one thing; no one in America is getting beheaded over old Tannenbaum. But now, as often as not, your kids' Christmas performances at school have morphed into Winter Concerts or December Plays. Nativity scenes are disappearing from the village green. School administrators and town councils across the land have eagerly placed Kwanzaa right up there on bulletin boards and holiday displays alongside Christmas and Hanukkah and the Winter Solstice. The message is clear: These "holidays" are all interchangeable, and your "faith tradition" is really just a matter of taste.

But Christmas is singular (and as you'll read, it's also very much a matter of taste). It's intrinsic to the American character, both in the gauche, free-market sense, and also the sense of self-image. Everyone wants to believe himself to be charitable and peaceable and kind. Christmas glorifies God, sure. But it also exalts the great American traditions of consumerism and commercialization in wholly acceptable ways. It's about giving, but it's a time to be okay with receiving, too. You can't beat Christmas with a stick. Yet beat it some do.

What Jonah's essay started me thinking about was not the metaphorical war itself, but about the people fighting it. What's going on inside the folks who spend their days and nights badgering—and suing—city hall to dismantle the town's Nativity display? Or bullying the elementary school principal into barring the choir from singing "Joy to the World" at the Holiday Festival? (These are real-life examples, by the way.)

On the one hand, I'm tempted to lump these folks in with Madalyn Murray O'Hair, the founder of the group American Atheists, who spent much of her life campaigning and filing lawsuits against Christmas. O'Hair was such a hard case that when one of her sons converted to Christianity as an adult, she announced, "I repudiate him entirely and completely for now and all times. One could call this a postnatal abortion on the part of a mother." Even Scrooge would have looked at O'Hair and thought, *Whoa.* But surely the people who want to get rid of Christmas can't all be as sour as she was. And even if they are, someone that broken deserves more pity than contempt.

Because when you renounce Christmas, you're also giving up the look on your kid's face when he opens the Tickle Me Elmo he's been dreaming of. You're giving up the intangible yet unmistakable (and sometimes slightly uncomfortable) sense of goodwill you feel toward complete strangers once Starbucks breaks out the red cups and gingerbread lattes. You're giving up the traditions that—however secular or ridiculous they may be—have become our own little Christmas miracles.

And of course, you're giving up Jesus, too. In recent years there's been a campaign to "put Christ back in Christmas." But in truth, no matter how many lawsuits you file, you can't take Him out of it. Even in the midst of the most consumerized, commercialized Christmas, He's there. On the cross, in the manger, and in the middle of Costco. And as P. J. O'Rourke will show you, God loves commerce. It says so in the Bible.

It's up to the Christmas virtues to fight the big, cosmic battles for the salvation of mankind. *The Christmas Virtues* is about fighting smaller battles. With family members. Over turkey and stockings and childhood grievances. On Christmas, you show up to honor the Holy Family while rolling your eyes at your own.

You'll find the thread of family running through this book. And not just in places where you'd expect it—like Matt Labash's guide on how to survive the holidays with your extended relations, even when they start throwing Bibles at one another. (No, really.) In his chapter on the ghosts of his Christmases past, Toby Young grapples with his late father's quirks (he often invited random strangers he met on Christmas morning to dinner later that night—but didn't always remember to show up himself). Steve Hayes recalls his parents' cheerfully sadistic game of having the kids wait at the top of the stairs to take family photos before they were allowed to come down and open Santa's bounty (a tradition that Steve has now gleefully shared with / imposed on his own children).

Elsewhere in the book you'll see that if they had a sense of humor, the anti-Christmas crusaders might actually enjoy some of the weirdness created by the secularization of Christmas. Andrew Ferguson, for instance, gets a jump on his time in purgatory every year by spending his daily commute contemplating the finer points of Christmas music on the holiday radio station. It turns out that many modern Christmas tunes are only tangentially about Christmas. For example, when Mariah Carey—Andy thinks of her as the "Yuletide sex kitten"—belts out that all she wants for Christmas is "you," she isn't talking about the Christ Child.

Some of our Christmas trappings have actually become opportunities for secular scolding. In his chapter on Christmas cards, Joe Queenan observes that, for some people, the holiday card is now an occasion to press political convictions (not to mention personal tribulations) on you. And for you to judge them for it. As Joe writes, "Christmas cards force us to confront things about our friends that we would prefer not to deal with." Like the fact that some of them choose to send cards from UNICEF or Doctors Without Borders—which is even more offensive than sending the kind of cheap, generic cards you get in lots of a hundred at the dollar store.

Yet the same condescending cards that make the Yuletide infuriating also keep it from being transactional. You can't throw these things away, no matter how strange you find it that your second-cousin-not-enough-times-removed sent a picture of her awkward teenagers dressed up as reindeer. Family tradition dictates that they must be taped to the window.

Most of us have a favorite Christmas song that conjures a sentimental tear on cold winter nights. Or a particular ritual for trimming the tree—not to mention a fervent conviction on the question of white versus colored lights. Or a cherished, so-bad-it's-good movie we pop in every December. Sonny Bunch, in an epic disquisition on Christmas cinema, makes a compelling case for the best Christmas film of all time—not because it's a cinematic masterpiece, but simply because watching it is a family tradition.

God gives us Christmas, but it's our families that create the traditions we hold in our hearts. I hope that the stories in this little book become part of your Christmas tradition and that you'll come back to them every year.

❧

My most beloved Christmas tradition is an Advent reading of W. H. Auden's Christmas oratorio, "For the Time Being." Like everything else good in my life, this slim, transcendent volume came to me through my wife. The first Christmas we were married, she read the poem to me as we sat on the futon, alone in our small apartment, a few feet from a tiny Christmas tree.

She reads it to me every year at Christmastime, though our tradition has evolved somewhat. We have an actual house now, with a fireplace and ceilings high enough for a proper tree. And before we get to Auden, we begin by reading "The Night before Christmas" to the kids. Then, after we've tucked them off to bed and straightened up the kitchen, we settle in on an actual sofa by the fire. And I keep a baby monitor next to me while she reads.

A sprawling dramatic poem, penned in the darkest moments of World War II, "For the Time Being" could just as easily describe our own difficulty in comprehending—or even recognizing—the presence of divinity in our postmodern world:

> . . . It's as if
> We had left our house for five minutes to mail a letter,
> And during that time the living room had changed places
> With the room behind the mirror over the fireplace.
> . . . I mean
> That the world of space where events re-occur is still there,

Only now it's no longer real; the real one is nowhere
Where time never moves and nothing can ever happen.

Like *The Christmas Virtues*—well, maybe not exactly like it—
the poem tells the Nativity story from the viewpoints of multiple
narrators, from the humble shepherds to the Wise Men, Mary
and Joseph, from the Four Faculties to a liberal King Herod—
who comes across less as a villain than a put-upon, and darkly
funny, politician. (As Adam Gopnik once observed, Auden's
Herod "mourns the loss of rational consensus in the face of
feckless sectarianism." Here's Herod lamenting that "civilisa-
tion must be saved even if this means sending for the military,
as I suppose it does. How dreary." This, as he's ordering the
Massacre of the Innocents.)

In roughly fifteen hundred lines, Auden captures the meaning and nuance of Christmas: loss and love, misery and mercy,
rejection and redemption. The poem reflects on everything
that had to happen in order for Christmas to come about:
Mary's heart-stopping *fiat*, Joseph's heart-rending doubt, the
alignment of stars and planets, and humanity's need for deliv-
erance. One of the things I love about it is that unlike most
Christmas stories, it doesn't have an entirely happy ending. It
closes not with the miracle, but with an ambivalence bordering
on recalcitrance:

Well, so that is that. Now we must dismantle the tree,
Putting the decorations back into their cardboard boxes—
Some have got broken—and carrying them up to the attic.
The holly and the mistletoe must be taken down and burnt,
And the children got ready for school. There are enough
Left-overs to do, warmed-up, for the rest of the week—
Not that we have much appetite, having drunk such a lot,
Stayed up so late, attempted—quite unsuccessfully—

To love all of our relatives, and in general
Grossly overestimated our powers. Once again
As in previous years we have seen the actual Vision and failed
To do more than entertain it as an agreeable
Possibility, once again we have sent Him away,
Begging though to remain His disobedient servant,
The promising child who cannot keep His word for long.
The Christmas Feast is already a fading memory,
And already the mind begins to be vaguely aware
Of an unpleasant whiff of apprehension at the thought
Of Lent and Good Friday which cannot, after all, now
Be very far off. But for the time being, here we all are. . . .

Here we all are. It is at this point every year, as Advent and our annual reading draw to a close, that I remember that "For the Time Being" isn't the perfect Christmas poem. It's the perfect after-Christmas poem. It describes not the magic I felt on the Christmas mornings of my childhood, but the real Christmas. The Christmas that only grown-ups can know:

. . . The streets
Are much narrower than we remembered; we had forgotten
The office was as depressing as this. To those who have seen
The Child, however dimly, however incredulously,
The Time Being is, in a sense, the most trying time of all.
For the innocent children who whispered so excitedly
Outside the locked door where they knew the presents to be
Grew up when it opened.

Parents the world over dread the post-Christmas letdown as much as they enjoy the pre-Christmas buildup. But the human condition is that we must always return to the present, to the time in which, as the Second Wise Man bemoans, "we anticipate or remember but never are." Because I'm a natural Eeyore, this hits me where I live. "The Time Being" is, in *every* sense, the most trying time of all.

And it's at this moment, every year, that my wife reminds me that Auden wasn't quite finished:

> He is the Way.
> Follow Him through the land of Unlikeliness;
> You will see rare beasts, and have unique adventures.
>
> He is the Truth.
> Seek Him in the Kingdom of Anxiety;
> You will come to a great city that has expected your return
> for years.
>
> He is the Life.
> Love Him in the World of the Flesh;
> And at your marriage all its occasions shall dance for joy.

Auden's prescription for the grown-up, existential longing we feel for what has just passed by us—what we have barely glimpsed, let alone grasped—is an invitation to joy. It's simple in expression, but difficult in execution: Follow, seek, and love.

Difficult, but not impossible.

The hour is late and Santa is on his way, but allow me to offer a parting thought about ontology.

I was, at least at the start, somewhat ambivalent about fatherhood. I do not have anything like a Hallmark view of the vocation; I experience it as much as a job I'm called to do as a blessing I happily enjoy (though, of course, those things are often one and the same).

Yet one of the things fatherhood made extremely clear to me is the truth that the act of creation is inherently an act of love. I don't have one of those stories about how the day my first child was born was the happiest day of my life and blah, blah, blah. For me, it really wasn't that way. The birth of our first kid was wrapped up in an enormous amount of anxiety and fear. Yet through that cloud, I suddenly realized that the creation of his life was the greatest act of love I would ever be part of. Simultaneously, I was overwhelmed by how much God must love me—must love all of us—to have made us.

Then I was hit, like a freight train, with a real, palpable understanding of how much God must love us to have given His Son to be born in this world, too.

These are the truths that became dazzlingly clear to me as I sat waiting for the nurse to bring me into the operating room where my wife would deliver our son.

These are the miracles I treasure most each Christmas.

CHAPTER 1

The Christmas Spirit
In Defense of Ebenezer Scrooge

Rob Long

THERE ARE LOTS of different editions of the book. Some of them are large and ornately illustrated, with woodcuts and curlicue letters; some of them pocket-sized and printed on cheap paper with smudgy ink. Either way, by the middle of page one or the top of page two of Charles Dickens' misunderstood paean to the Christmas season, you've got the basic gist.

And the point of *A Christmas Carol* is this: Most people are irritating and selfish, especially around Christmastime. They march around in gaudy cheerfulness, braying good wishes to everyone within earshot, repeating the tiresome pieties of the season—Happy Holidays!—and pester friends and relations and employers for all sorts of favors and boons and cash money gifts, which, when firmly refused on the principle—and this is important, so please pay attention to it—that *money does not grow on trees* and that *hey, some of us around here work for a living*, they recoil in horror as if somehow the poor, hardworking, petitioned, and beleaguered employer is out of step with the sentiment of the moment. As if it's the grasping, gimme-gimme outstretched hand of the petitioner that is somehow the true embodiment of the Christmastide.

I am aware, just so you know, that my personal interpretation of the opening pages of *A Christmas Carol* isn't widely shared. But that doesn't make it wrong.

Let me put it another way. For those of you who are fans of the New Testament, recall that in Luke 2:2, we're told that Caesar Augustus issued a decree that "a census should be taken of the entire Roman world." Rome being Rome, it's fair to assume that this wasn't a spur-of-the-moment decree. There were probably signs and rumblings and bureaucratic indications that such a ruling was coming down the pike, and any thinking person from the house and line of David knew that this meant traveling with a pregnant wife all the way to Bethlehem. You'd think such a person would, oh, I don't know, *make reservations.*

Even back then—really, honestly, the *Ur*-moment of Christmas—there was this sense of, *Oh well. Someone will sort this out for us. It's Christmas, after all!*

And when the "someone" has a fully committed Bethlehem Inn because a lot of type-A plan-aheaders either got an earlier start or *took responsibility for themselves,* we're supposed to see this as a virtue of . . . the parents who didn't, and then have to deliver the baby in the barn! With the dirty animals all gathered around! With the smells and the fleas and the whatnot! Unbelievable!

I am aware, just so you know, that my personal interpretation of Luke 2:2–38 isn't widely shared, either. But that doesn't make it wrong.

I dwell on the opening pages of *A Christmas Carol* and my nagging sense that both Mary and Joseph needed to get it together, parenting-wise, because when we read Dickens' masterpiece—and we're reading it wrong, in my opinion—or when we think about the First Christmas in the Gospels, we're not paying attention to the important part of the story. We're missing the True Meaning, which is: Getting presents is important. Whatever else Christmas is, it's a lot about *receiving.*

Let us return to the text.

In the opening sequences of *A Christmas Carol*—which in a way is a kind of secular gospel story for the secular Christmas—hardworking and thrifty Scrooge is bent over his desk delivering value to his clients. In addition, by restricting the use of coal in his office fireplace, he's also doing his part to clean up London's then-notoriously poor air quality. Not that he gets any credit for that, but moving on.

His nephew enters, possibly drunk, to invite him to Christmas dinner, with a series of blatantly passive-aggressive statements that no sane person could misinterpret. Scrooge then accurately assesses the utility of the Christmas holiday thus:

"What's Christmastime to you but a time for paying bills without money; a time for finding yourself a year older, but not an hour richer; a time for balancing your books and having every item in 'em through a round dozen of months presented dead against you? If I could work my will," says Scrooge indignantly, "every idiot who goes about with 'Merry Christmas' on his lips should be boiled with his own pudding and buried with a stake of holly through his heart. He should!"

Strong words, yes. But that doesn't make him wrong.

And then, moments later, in walk two do-gooders of the most shifty sort—neither, let's be frank, carries any identification or offers to prove his affiliation with any certified tax-exempt 501(c)(3) institution; I mean, these guys could be *anyone,* and they demand money from Scrooge because—and this is what gets me—he *has* it and other people *need* it. Scrooge quite reasonably replies with a slightly crude rejoinder—remember, Dickens is writing this one hundred years before Friedrich Hayek's magisterial post-Scrooge exegesis *The Road to Serfdom*—that boils down to, *Hey! I pay my taxes.*

What happens after that is well known. Scrooge is visited by three ghosts—the Ghosts of Christmases Past, Present, and Future—and by the end of his ordeal he's been transformed. We glimpse him at the close of the book giddy and rosy-cheeked—

tipsy on wine and generosity, full of Christmas spirit and bursting with a new and fuller heart. What we're supposed to think is this: that everyone *Else* around Scrooge had the *Right* spirit, the right Christmas attitude, and that the three ghostly visitations were a kind of Victorian spectral therapy—highly successful at that—in getting Ebenezer Scrooge with the program.

To which I say: Humbug.

Who, exactly, in the early pages of the book offers to give Scrooge anything? Sure, his nephew offers him the dubious pleasure of a dinner, but with company like that, Scrooge was right to prefer his porridge and his ale. In the enormous constellation of irritating characters in the Dickens universe, Scrooge's nephew looms large and bright. He is clearly one of those people who keeps tapping you when he talks. *Hey, hey, hey, pay attention to me!* And he's one of those guys who keeps telling the same story over again. *I'm telling you, Uncle Scrooge! It was hilarious! Hi-lar-i-ous! We were screaming. Seriously.*

Who wants to have dinner with that?

And then people come in and want his money. And then his employee wants time off. No one—*no one*—offers to give *him* anything. Scrooge and the world are at a standoff. He's a miser, yes. But the rest of the world is withholding, too. He refuses to budge, but so does everyone else.

The picture of his life, painted in images and ghostly time travels, is one of sadness and loneliness and rejection. These days, we'd call it what it is: depression. But back then, surely, in the sentimental and emotional Victorian era, when people were fainting and shrinking and collapsing from consumption and heartbreak, what's remarkable is how callously the world treated the younger Ebenezer Scrooge, how stingy it was with its gifts and its love. Scrooge, in almost every respect, is exactly whom David Copperfield or Nicholas Nickleby would have turned into, without the lucky breaks that Charles Dickens doled out to them.

Still, Scrooge wakes up full of the Christmas spirit, radiant with joy and laughter, and showers gifts on everyone in his circle. To which we're supposed to say, *It's about time.*

And yet, in the final chapter, when Scrooge sends the little street urchin off to buy a turkey—"The one as big as me?"—for the Cratchits, it takes a certain kind of selfish, smug, utter misunderstanding of the point of Christmas not to ask, *Hey, did anyone ever buy Scrooge a turkey?*

We know the answer to that. The answer is no. And then we wonder why he seems like such a jerk.

Put it another way: When, after days of hard travel across desert and who-knows-what, the Wise Men arrive at the bedside of the Savior—the Gospel of Matthew, thankfully, has by this time transferred the baby from the livestock keep to the house, so I guess someone from child services stepped in and got things sorted out—they come bearing gifts. And we know what those gifts are because—and please pay attention here—*gifts are important.*

Gifts are not superficial or silly or a sign of greed or secret agendas. Gifts—especially expensive ones like gold, frankincense, and whatever myrrh is—are a perfect way to say things that are hard for people to say. Things like, *I love you.* And, *You are important to me.* And, *I want you to smell good.* And, *This almost put me in the poorhouse to get, but I did it because you are my everything.*

The trouble is, when you reach a certain age, you stop getting Christmas presents. Good ones, anyway. Someone will give you socks, of course, or something equally last-minute, but when you turn the corner on thirty or thirty-five, suddenly children start to appear in the family and Christmas becomes all about them.

I hate that.

And not because I don't like kids. I love kids. But I also love presents—especially the smaller, heavier ones that sit under the tree and positively glow with the promise of high-value, expensive stuff. Or those that are wrapped in paper exclusive to some very high-end emporium. Back when I often wore neckties to work, I especially loved seeing slender orange boxes under the tree with my name on them. It meant, unmistakably, that someone was giving me a necktie from Hermès, which fulfills all of the major criteria for a perfect present: it's expensive, it's silky, I can wear it, and it's expensive.

Once, as a joke, my brother put a new plastic Bic pen inside a Hermès necktie box, wrapped it up, and placed it under the tree without comment. He had a good laugh on Christmas morning. I did not join in. A Bic pen, as I'm sure I made clear, fulfills zero of the criteria for a perfect present: it's cheap, it's plastic, I cannot wear it, and it's cheap.

But I'm old now. And I know the score: When Christmas rolls around, I know I'm not going to get anything that doesn't come from a bin that's close to the cashier. I sit at my tall scrivener's desk, creating value for my clients, and I am not asked what I want. I am told, instead, what to buy.

And I know this isn't my most attractive trait—although honesty compels me to admit that it's also not my least attractive trait—but I like getting presents. As made clear in my textual analysis of the Gospels of Luke, Matthew, and Dickens, I believe that giving and getting presents is a very important part of the Christmas story. Maintaining the sacredness of that transaction—beyond the Santa years, into adulthood and dotage—keeps us all from falling into the Scrooge trap.

Last year, though, I had an idea. I got all of the adults in the family to agree to a "Secret Santa" scheme. We'd put our names in a hat, draw a name apiece, and buy a gift for the person whose name was drawn. "But something substantial," I whined to everyone. "Something heavy and expensive and fulfilling the criteria I've been talking about for years." They all nodded. They were familiar, they told me, with my criteria.

And we'd keep it all secret until Christmas Day. Hence the "secret" part of Secret Santa. They all agreed, which surprised me, because frankly I think everyone in my family enjoys winding me up every Christmas. It's a cruelty that only close family can indulge in, because only they know your secret weaknesses and private character flaws. A cheap pen, a pair of socks—my family knew that I wanted something more, and that I looked upon the happy children on Christmas morning who were laden with toys and games and fun stuff with a mixture of jealousy and rage. They liked watching me pretend that I wasn't and knew that it was just a matter of time until I erupted into one of the more powerful monologues delivered by Scrooge on page one or two of *A Christmas Carol*. Depending on your edition.

Somehow, though, I convinced them to enthusiastically embrace the Secret Santa scheme. Perhaps I wasn't the only one who missed getting a high-end present under the tree. Maybe I was just more honest about it.

So I happily went about the business of Secret Santa: I wrote everyone's name down on a piece of paper, found a hat, tossed the papers inside, and we made the draw. Everyone seemed to be happy with who they got. "It's secret," I reminded everyone. "Don't tell anyone whose name you drew."

About thirty minutes later, though, my brother looked up suddenly. A terrible thought had occurred.

"Rob," he asked, "did you just write your own name down on every piece of paper?"

I was outraged.

"What kind of person do you think I am?" I shouted.

"The kind of person who would like to find a pile of gifts under the tree all for himself."

In a way, it's touching that he knew me so well. Because, of course, that's exactly what I had done.

So we drew again—this time, in the proper manner—and a new family tradition was born. That, in a way, was my gift to my family. It was a nice one, and I know they appreciated it. But it doesn't compare to the largest turkey in the shop window. Surely there's someone in your life, right now, who would like that?

Surely there's someone in your life, right now, who is a Scrooge but doesn't want to be.

CHAPTER 2

The Commercialization
of Christmas

God Moves (the Merchandise) in a Mysterious Way

P. J. O'Rourke

DESPITE WHAT you may have heard, the commercialization of Christmas is a virtue, a Christian virtue. To understand the virtuousness of a commercialized Christmas, start with commerce rather than Christ. It predates Him.

The Three Wise Men of the East shopped at established markets for gold, frankincense, and myrrh. These markets were not founded on the expectation of trading opportunities in Christ Child futures.

Commerce has existed from the beginning of civilization, in particular from the beginning of *our* civilization, when we were dragged out of barbarism, protesting all the way, by the Ten Commandments. ("The good news is, I got Him down to ten. The bad news is, adultery's still on the list," I think Moses said.)

The Eighth Commandment is about microeconomics, or what people who aren't economists call the daily grind: "Thou shalt not steal." This signifies that there are goods and services that are neither held in common nor collectively owned by the state. Otherwise the Eighth Commandment would be, "Thou shalt not vote Republican." God proclaims private property rights. But without commerce—without the capacity to trade in the goods and services we own—private property rights are insignificant and trivial. God made the world. "He created it not in vain" (Isaiah 45:18). So our commercial ways and means matter to God. We aren't a divine unprofitable hobby or foolish pastime. We're not God's selfie sticks.

Yes, Christmas is merchandized. (Selfie sticks with bows on their handles will protrude from many a Christmas stocking.) But the Old Testament devotes more attention to the mercantile than to the messianic—more attention, that is, in a workaday and quantitative sense. And commerce is nothing if not quotidian and measurable.

The Old Testament prophesies the coming of Jesus, of course. The Bible is a prophetic, awe-inspiring, sacred text. But it's also a book of rules for everyday life. And very little in this rulebook indicates that life should be all Lent and no Christmas morning with presents under the tree.

Indeed, once God is done blowing His top at Adam and Eve for being fruitarian slackers getting their information from the Tweet of Knowledge, He gives them some nice presents. "Unto Adam also and to his wife did the Lord God make coats of skins, and clothed them." The first Blackglama advertisement. What becomes a legend most?

According to *Strong's Exhaustive Concordance* the word *buy* and its derivatives occur 108 times in the Bible, *sell* 132 times, and *prosper* 93 times, mostly in a "Go ye up, and prosper" context. And as Adam Smith noticed, "going ye up" prospers nobody unless there's commerce—conducted in the silver and gold that are mentioned 816 times in the Bible.

Chapter ten of 1 Kings goes on for twenty-nine verses about the benefits of free trade and supply-side economics during the Solomon administration in Israel. Some of the descriptions are mouthwatering. "And the king made silver to be in Jerusalem as stones, and cedars made he to be as the sycamore trees that are in the vale, for abundance." (Assuming what makes your mouth water is investment-grade bullion and a mansion full of custom-made, walk-in cedar closets. I've checked the *Wall Street Journal*'s "Mansion" section. Sycamore closets are not in demand.)

Israelites engaging in successful commerce must have been—given King Solomon's reputation for sagacity—wise. True, Solomon's later reign was troubled. "Second-term curse" we'd call it. But that had to do with seven hundred wives and Solomon paying his respects to the abomination of Moloch, not business. (Although representing seven hundred wives divorcing a man who "exceeded all the kings of the earth in riches" would have done wonders for a tenth-century BC attorney's billable hours.)

The word *commerce* enters the English language during the late sixteenth century and is defined in Dr. Johnson's *Dictionary* as "exchange of one thing for another." This is certainly what Jesus is telling us to do when He says to turn the other cheek. To illustrate usage, Johnson quotes from John Dryden's poem *Annus Mirabilis*, which celebrates all the wonderful things God provided to England in the twelve months spanning 1665 and 1666: victory over the Dutch at the Battle of Lowestoft; London's Great Fire sparing Westminster and being mostly confined to thirteen thousand charred hovels in the slums; and the various felicities of King Charles II's reign as the Merry Monarch, such as, maybe (the poem is 1,216 lines long, and I confess I haven't read the whole thing) the king having Cavalier King Charles Spaniels named after him.

But in the stanza from *Annus Mirabilis* that Dr. Johnson quotes, a Christmas season peace-on-earth / goodwill-to-men case for the virtues of commercialization is made:

> Instructed ships shall sail to quick commerce,
> By which remotest regions are ally'd;
> Which makes one city of the universe,
> Where some may gain, and all may be suppy'd.

But, wait: "Where some may gain." *There's* the catch by which "henceforth thou shalt catch men."

Jesus is notoriously tough on the rich. That Matthew 19:24—"easier . . . than for a rich man to enter into the kingdom of God"—is tough stuff. It leaves most of us hoping there's a miniature breed of dromedary out there somewhere and that the Central Park Cleopatra's Needle has, buried in its foundation, an eye of commensurate size. And we're not the only ones. In the very next line Matthew reports, "When his disciples heard it, they were exceedingly amazed, saying, Who then can be saved?" And then Jesus relents (sighing, I suppose), "With men this is impossible; but with God all things are possible."

Of course, he would say that. Because Jesus was a rich kid. Christ, the Christmas presents he got!

There was nothing Scrooge-like about the Three Wise Men. We can assume they each brought the little Lord Jesus at least a *mina* of gold or frankincense or myrrh. A mina was a common measurement of weight in the ancient Middle East, equal to 1.25 pounds. Frankincense is a type of incense or room freshener that was probably more valuable in a smelly AD 1 manger than it is now. It currently sells on Amazon for $16.88 an ounce. Myrrh is a perfume, antiseptic, and ingredient in analgesic liniment, thus also precious in a smelly manger. An ounce of myrrh goes for $14.75. The spot price on the London Gold Market is, as of this writing, $1,096.23 per ounce.

So Jesus got $22,556.35 for his birthday. A nice piece of change, but not Jeff Bezos money—until you do 2,015 years of Consumer Price Index adjustment for inflation. In the time of Christ, a day's pay for an unskilled laborer was one denarius. It's no use trying to calculate a simple Travelex dollar/denarius exchange rate. The nature of goods and services has changed too much. After all, King Solomon himself couldn't afford an iPhone. And nowadays where would you get a vestal virgin at any price?

Better to think in terms of a Roman Empire minimum wage. The U.S. federal minimum wage is $7.25 an hour. An eight-hour day gets us fifty-eight dollars. The best information we have about pay rates in the Roman Empire comes from the Imperial "Edict of Maximum Prices," which included the maximum prices for labor. The edict was issued in AD 301 by the emperor Diocletian (a big persecutor of Christians, by the way). It took four workdays for an unskilled Roman to make enough money to buy a *modius* of wheat, a dry measure equaling 9.2 quarts. There are thirty-two quarts in a bushel, and therefore 3.5 *modii*. American wheat is selling for $4.68 a bushel. Which means that for locavores shopping at the farmers' markets, a *modius* of wheat will set you back $1.35.

So in the Roman Empire the minimum wage was thirty-two cents a day. A bent pin and pocket lint per hour. Nothing and not enough of it. If in those days "he that reapeth receiveth wages" got thirty-two cents for a day's work and now we get fifty-eight dollars, then what Jesus started life with wasn't twenty-two thousand dollars and change—it was $4 million. Jesus, Joseph, and Mary didn't "flee into Egypt," they booked a suite at the Hilton Sharm El Sheikh Fayrouz Resort on the Red Sea.

Which is a nice place to celebrate Christmas as long as terrorists stay off the property, and even if the Coptic Christian calendar does make Santa do everything all over again on January 7.

So where did Christ's money go? There's no record of its disposal. Of course there isn't. "Take heed that ye do not your alms before men, to be seen of them" (Matthew 6:1). And here lies the origin of our doing-double-duty-in-Egypt Santa Claus.

Santa is the polite (and, I would argue, sacred) fiction that allows us to obey—at least with the little children we suffer to come unto us—the teaching of Jesus that "when thou doest

alms, let not thy left hand know what thy right hand is doing."
(It's attempting to assemble a WowWee Robosapien X shipped
to our house at 11:00 p.m. on Christmas Eve with instructions
in Chinese.)

Christmas is the time when we come closest to success at giving more than we receive. Last Christmas I received a pipe rack
made in woodcraft class (I smoke cigars), an atrocious necktie depicting a neon crèche (which I had to wear to midnight
Mass), and a pair of fluffy bunny slippers. My wife gave me a
present that was wonderful and perfect. (She'll read this book.)

"Some may gain" from the making and selling of these gifts
to give. I don't mind. God bless the people trying to earn their
daily bread stitching fluffy bunny slippers. Jesus doesn't mind
either. A young man seeking holiness asked Jesus, "What lack
I yet?" (Matthew 19:20–22). Jesus replied, "If thou wilt be perfect, go and sell that thou hast, and give to the poor."

This presupposes there is a rightful "that" that is rightfully
"hast." And Christ says "sell"—not "allow to be expropriated or
nationalized." Nor did He make a convert. Nor did He mean
to. Christ is Lord. The Lord knows all, including what was in
the heart of the questioner. "When the young man heard that
saying, he went away sorrowful: for he had great possessions."

Christ Himself practiced commerce, "exchange of one thing
for another." He exchanged faith for works in His healings, and
works for faith, "that ye may know the Son of man hath power
on earth." He wasn't even averse to commercial ad campaigns
of a viral marketing type: "Neither do men light a candle and
put it under a bushel." (Which would also be a fire hazard.)

In the parable of the Talents, the rich capitalist, "reaping
where I sowed not," isn't a villain, but a metaphor for God. The
servants who made a return on the money they were managing
(a 100 percent return!) were rewarded in a way that, if the story
appeared in the *Huffington Post* instead of the New Testament,

would be titled "Wall Street Bonuses Soar While Middle-Class Income Stagnates." But the servant who "was afraid, and went and hid thy talent in the earth," that is, who bought thirty-day T-bills with an negative yield when matched against inflation, was sacked: "Cast ye the unprofitable servant into outer darkness: There shall be weeping and gnashing of teeth."

Nobody's perfect. Jesus said, "Why callest thou me good? There is none good but one, that is, God." And Christmas is not the feast of perfection. Even the date of Christmas Day is imperfect—a fuzzy approximation of when Christ was born. Astronomers, pondering the "star in the east," think the heavenly body that "stood over where the young child was" may have been the conjunction of Saturn and Jupiter in October, 7 BC; or perhaps the conjunction of Jupiter and Venus in June, 2 BC. Biblical scholars note that the shepherds were "keeping watch over their flock by night" and thus peg the birth of Jesus during lambing season in March.

According to my grandmother, "If 'ifs' and 'buts' were fruits and nuts we'd have Christmas every day." And it seems we do, no matter the fact that we haven't been being "good for goodness' sake."

By the by, that modern Christmas carol—"Santa Claus Is Coming to Town"—was written by commercial songwriters John Frederick Coots and Haven Gillespie and was first sung on commercial radio by Eddie Cantor—in between commercials. Commercially, "Santa Claus Is Coming to Town" was a big success, selling one hundred thousand copies of sheet music and thirty thousand records within twenty-four hours of its release.

Tidings of comfort and joy are unnecessary for those who are joyfully comfortable because their conscience is clear. But the rest of us could use some merriment. And Christ joins in, saying, "The Son of man came eating and drinking, and they say, Behold a man gluttonous, and a winebibber, a friend of publicans and sinners." Publican (from the Latin *publicum*, public revenue) is usually defined as "tax collector," but a better translation would be "petty government official." So Jesus was having dinner with Ted Kennedy!

Yet something in the dark heart of fallen humanity makes us protest against the commerce of Christmas, its trade in good things and good feelings. This prejudice dates back to the Dark Ages—the 1950s—when Tom Lehrer recorded "A Christmas Carol":

> Hark the *Herald Tribune* sings,
> Advertising wondrous things.
>
> God rest ye merry, merchants,
> May you make the Yuletide pay.
>
> Angels we have heard on high
> Tell us to go out and buy!
>
> So let the raucous sleigh bells jingle,
> Hail our dear old friend Kris Kringle,
> Driving his reindeer across the sky.
> Don't stand underneath when they fly by.

There were objections to Christmas fun even before that. In AD 245 Origen of Alexandria was against celebrating Christ's birthday because he maintained that Scripture mentions only sinners, such as Pharaoh, celebrating birthdays. (Genesis 40:20–22 describes Pharaoh having his chief baker hanged at his birthday party—chief bakers should, perhaps, steer a prudent course between tact and accuracy when exposing the birthday boy's age.)

After the Protestant Reformation, some Christians, including the English Puritans, condemned celebrating Christmas because they considered it a Catholic invention. Christmas decorations were the "trappings of popery" and holiday finery the "rags of the Beast."

In 1647 Cromwell enacted legislation against Christmas festivities. Pro-Christmas rioting broke out in several cities.

> O bring us some figgy pudding
> Or we'll burn down your house!

Colonial America's Puritans deplored chestnuts roasting on an open fire, Jack Frost nipping at your nose, Yuletide carols being sung by a choir, etc. Christmas was banned in Boston from 1659 to 1681. Among the manifold qualities of God, let us not forget irony: "Banned in Boston" would eventually become one of the great American commercial enticements—so much so that book publishers, playwrights, and movie producers lined up to have their products banished from Beantown.

As late as 1860, Christmas was a legal holiday in just fourteen states. But now, thank God, Christians everywhere have come to their senses. They embrace the spirit of Christmas with open arms. And open wallets. The holiday season commences with one of the great American holy days: Black Friday.

So powerful is the spirit of Christmas that even Ebenezer Scrooge embraced it at last. And, as befit a "squeezing, wrenching, grasping, clutching, covetous old sinner," Scrooge celebrated the spirit of Christmas in a thoroughly commercial way.

Read, if you can through your tears, the final stave of *A Christmas Carol*, the chapter where Scrooge awakes after visits by the ghosts of lonely Christmas Past, grimly Christmas Present, and dead-buried-and-forgotten Christmas Yet to Come. Scrooge then buys a prize turkey as big as the errand boy, tips the errand boy munificently, makes a large cash donation to the poor, gives Bob Cratchit a handsome raise, and pays for Tiny Tim's medical treatment rather than abandon young Timothy to the tender mercies of Victoriacare.

As the electronic devices of obscure purpose that Santa will bring our kids remind us, the commercialization of Christmas isn't a bug; it's a feature.

> God moves in a mysterious way
> His wonders to beget;
> He plants His footsteps in the mall
> And rides the Internet.

CHAPTER 3

Season's Greetings!
Ten Simple Rules for Sending Christmas Cards

Joe Queenan

CHRISTMAS IS A TIME to be joyful and thankful and optimistic and forward-looking, even if you grew up in Philadelphia. Christmas is a time to count our blessings and think how lucky we are not to be living in Kabul or engaged to one of the Kardashians. It is a time to think about how much we love our friends and how much we enjoy hearing from them at this time of year.

And then they go and ruin everything by sending us Christmas cards.

Christmas cards are supposed to be a source of untrammeled joy. They're supposed to hark back to a simpler, more innocent time when the herald angels sang and we three kings of Orient were. But this is no longer true. Today, Christmas cards are fraught with unsettling undertones and even more unsettling overtones.

For starters, there are religious overtones, since we do not all share the same religion and some people belong to religions that don't even like the other religions. Then there are cultural overtones. There are political overtones. There are aesthetic undertones. Ultimately, Christmas cards are a Rorschach test that tell us more about our relationships than we would like to know. Christmas cards force us to confront things about our friends that we would prefer not to deal with.

You know what I'm talking about. Think of the deep disappointment you experience when you receive that flimsy white envelope with a crass, non-Yuletide Forever Stamp up in the corner. Often it has mud or caked cereal on it. Tearing it open, you find a sad, generic, graphically uninspiring "Holiday Greetings" card depicting a faded holly wreath or a cheap-looking candle. You recognize this as one of those mass-produced cards purchased in lots of sixty thousand at box stores, bearing the impersonal, one-size-fits-all message:

Happy Holidays
The Smiths

But that is not the worst. There is also the Christmas card with pictures of the ugly baby. The Christmas card with pictures of the ugly teens. The Christmas card with pictures of the ugly you. The professionally, stage-managed, incredibly expensive Christmas card ostensibly designed to make your family look less hideous. Is that Bigfoot in the center? Oh, sorry. That's your son, Skylar.

There are many other deeply unsatisfactory Christmas cards. There is the plangently atheistic, secular humanist Christmas card that screams "HELL WILL FREEZE OVER BEFORE I SEND YOU A CARD WITH THE WORDS 'MERRY CHRISTMAS' ON IT!" There is the Christmas card written in a language neither you nor the sender speaks. I understand *Feliz Navidad*. I understand *Joyeux Noël*. I do not understand *Prejeme Vam Vesele Vanoce*. Nor is there any reason I should.

Other offenders? The Christmas card with an ugly painting by Rouault. The Christmas card with the dachshund dressed up like an elf. The ironic Christmas card. The cheeky Christmas card. The card that is too cute for words. The card that is too enigmatic for words. The card that is too cute *and* too enigmatic for words—and that was too cute and too enigmatic for words last year, when you got exactly the same card. I am speaking, of course, of the Christmas card with the wolf kissing the caribou. Ugh.

Let us not forget the pinch-hitter Christmas card: The Christmas card that isn't really a Christmas card at all. The Monet painting of the lady with the parasol in high summer. Huh? Van Gogh's *Room at Arles*. Thanks, because Vinny the G really perks things up around the holidays. And, of course, the Edward Hopper card pressed into emergency service because the sender ran out of Christmas cards. The card depicts a morose, lonely usherette in an empty movie theater that is showing a film no one but Edward Hopper could possibly want to see. She seems to be whispering to herself, "As soon as I get off my shift, I'm going to go home and put my head in the oven."

Then comes the electronic Christmas card that makes your computer screen freeze. Or the electronic Christmas card that you don't dare open because you think it might contain a virus from Nigeria. Or the electronic Christmas card you don't open because you don't like electronic Christmas cards . . . because somebody else sent you the same electronic Christmas card last year. And because you can't hang an electronic card on the mantelpiece, which is the whole point of the exercise.

Many Christmas cards are designed with no other purpose than to gloat. *Merry Christmas from Tahiti! Holiday Greetings from Machu Picchu! Living the Dream in Maui! Just Another Day in Paradise at Hilton Head!* These cards sometimes depict Mrs. Claus in a beach hammock or Santa on a surfboard. As if Santa would ever sink so low.

And then there is my personal favorite—the unsigned Christmas card:

May the Miracle of Christmas Fill Your Days with Joy
[Unsigned]

Best Wishes for a Merry Holiday Season
The Masked Yuletide Reveler

Happy Holidays
Your Guess Is As Good As Mine

❧❀❧

A special place in hell is reserved for people who are supposed to be your closest friends, but who send you a generic Christmas card—and who then make things even worse by only signing their names. No "Looking forward to seeing you in the New Year." No "Sorry we didn't get together this year." No "I will always be grateful to you for warning me not to name my kid Rhiannon." No "I'll have that six grand back to you by Easter. With the vig." No nothing. Just the name.

Merry Christmas.
Patty and Larry

These are people you were in the service with. These are people you were in high school with. These are people you were in the ICU with. So how hard would it be to write a few measly words every December? How hard would it be to scrawl, "Still thinking about that Jerry Garcia solo at the Spectrum in 1974. Is it over yet?" or "Terrific news about your kid getting sprung from San Quentin!"

I could understand the terseness and economy if they were head of the International Monetary Fund, or chairman of the House Ways and Means Committee, or *Capo di tutti capi,* or the nurse manning the night shift in the emergency room at Mogadishu Metropolitan Hospital. But Patty and Larry are retired. The only thing they ever do is walk their dog and complain about their teeth. How hard would it be to scribble a few lines just to say howdy?

Finally, there is the dreaded Christmas letter. Christmas is a time to celebrate life. It is not a time to recapitulate all the bad things that happened to you in the past year. I hate it when I get the one-size-fits-all Christmas letter that starts off with:

> Whew! It's been a tough year for the Kinnear family. Jackson lost his job at the Assassin's Creed beta-testing center and Madison broke her hip rock climbing. Mingus and El Sparky got hit by a fire truck—same truck, same day—and Grandma has dementia. Sure hope your year was better than ours!!!

Couldn't this wait until January? Why do you have to go and spoil Christmas for everyone you know by trumpeting your bad news? Yes, I know that it's been a tough year for the Kinnear family. But it's been a tough year for a lot of families. And dude, this is not the venue. I lost five close friends in the past year, including my beloved brother-in-law, Tony. But I am not going to include this information in my annual Christmas letter, because I don't send out annual Christmas letters and neither did Tony. Tony had class.

❧❦❧

Let me make one thing perfectly clear: My own Christmas card-giving habits are impeccable. I buy beautiful, three-dimensional, pop-up cards with ebullient scenes of ice skaters in Central Park and adorable little choo-choo trains or Santa Claus in his sleigh with fabulous gifts tumbling out of his bag as Donner and Blitzen soar into the heavens. These cards cost about two bucks apiece at the Museum of Modern Art. I buy thirty-two of them every year and send them to my very closest friends and loved ones. The cards are so nice that people sometimes call me to say how nice they are.

But that doesn't mean that I send my lower-tier friends trash. The second echelon of friends—mostly colleagues I have stayed in contact with for many, many years—still get beautiful cards I purchase at the National Gallery or the Frick or the Metropolitan Museum of Art. Even the third-tier friends—neighbors, distant relatives, people who did me a favor many years ago—get decent cards. I never send out Christmas cards purchased at CVS or Dollar General or a yard sale. Those cards are repellent. I never send cards that other people are likely to send that same year. I never send cards that are soiled or faded. I put a lot of time and energy into this. I put my heart into it. Such as it is.

And how am I repaid? What do I get in return for my inexhaustible thoughtfulness and seemingly infinite largesse? I get cards that my friends got gratis from fund-raising mailers. Generic cards from UNICEF or the Fraternal Order of Police or the Sons of Tiramisu. Generic cards from causes I do not support. Generic cards from organizations I despise.

A long time ago I decided that I would not send people Christmas cards that came from charities. These cards look cheesy. Sending them means that you don't even value a person's friendship enough to go out and buy a decent card. It means that your friend or relative or child is an afterthought. It also means that you are cheap. Cheapness, I believe, is the only truly unforgivable crime. Cheapness makes the world a smaller, meaner place. Cheapness is grubby. I am always looking for a good reason to end friendships that have run their course. Cheapness qualifies. Cheapness is exactly like mass murder: It becomes your identity. Send me a cheap Christmas card where Santa looks drunk or Rudolph looks anorexic—after all I've done for you—and you are history. Think I'm kidding?

Try me.

I particularly dislike it when I receive a card from a preening, self-righteous organization I can't stand. Whenever I receive a card from the flamboyantly virtuous, I know the subtext: "Message: I care." Yeah, well, I don't.

I am speaking of the snooty, condescending Christmas card that upbraids you for not doing enough to make the world a better place, the Christmas card that comes with a hortatory or admonishing subliminal message. These cards are designed to scold, hector, browbeat, chide, taunt, belittle, and punish:

"I care about poor people, and that's why this card is from Doctors Without Borders. I care about the wide open spaces, and that's why this card is from the Sierra Club. I care about the lower primates, and that's why this card is from Save the Chimps. The truth is: I care about everything and everybody, and you don't.

"No, let me be even more specific: My card wishes you and your family happiness you do not even deserve because none of you have ever done anything for the whales, the manatee, the snow otter, the Sumatran flying serpent, or the polar bear. You have never done anything to save the rain forest or the deaf or the polar ice cap or the starving children of Darfur. You didn't do anything this year or any other year to stop baby seal slaughter or the routine torture of lab animals. If rodents could write, they would not even bother to send you a Christmas card. Considering how appalling you are, I think I'm being pretty generous and forgiving."

About thirty years ago I started hanging on to Christmas cards. Instead of tossing them in the trash after the holidays, I would stuff them in a filing cabinet in my office. Christmas cards, when accumulated over the years, provide a graphic history of our lives. Some of these cards are quite beautiful. Some of them are from friends who are no longer among the living. Some of them are from people I no longer like. One friend, whose card-sending program must be on automatic pilot, continues to send me a card every year, even though he did something so unforgivable that I will never speak to him again. I keep the cards, though. He is a friend who does not matter to me anymore. But he used to matter.

I look forward to receiving certain cards each year. A friend who used to be the librarian at the Museum of Modern Art sends exquisite cards. A friend from Detroit, long marooned in northern Florida with a sick parent, sends clever, funny cards. She spends a lot of time thinking about Christmas cards to take her mind off having to live in a part of the country that she loathes. About fifteen years ago I got on Pee-wee Herman's mailing list. Each year, he sends me the most amazing Christmas cards. They are collector's items. They look like they cost a fortune to produce. If everyone put as much effort into their Christmas cards as Pee-wee Herman, the world would be a better place.

Recently, I realized that there have been some egregious omissions from my Christmas card list. For years I have been sending cards to people who are just barely friends, but not to my doctor, my car mechanic, or the man who manages my money. Now I have changed that. I send them Christmas cards. I do not necessarily send them the very best cards. But I do send them a card.

Every year I give a small cash gift to the postman, the couple who clean my office building, and the people who work in the restaurant I visit several times each day. For the longest time I would enclose the gift in a card that I bought as a packaged set. Then one day it occurred to me that this one-size-fits-all approach was insulting. It wasn't so much that I was giving these people lower-quality Christmas cards. It was that I was giving them all the same card. And they knew it.

"So what?" a friend asked. "It's the money that counts."

No, it isn't. The money counts, sure, but so does the idea of honoring people who do a whole lot more for you during the year than most of your other friends do. So now I give my friends at the diner individual cards. Beautiful cards. Beautiful cards for beautiful people.

Do I keep a Christmas card ledger in which I monitor friends' Yuletide activities? Yes, I do. If friends fail to man up at Christmastime, they get trash-canned. Every year I go through my list of friends to decide whether to send them a Christmas card. If I do not send you a Christmas card, it does not necessarily mean that I no longer consider you a friend. It means that you did not consider me enough of a friend to send me a card last year, so I do not consider you enough of a friend to send you a card. Ever. People who do not call me for an entire year get purged from the list. People who send a card but merely sign their name at the bottom also get deep-sixed. It does not mean that I will stop being friends with them. It just means that they are not getting any more Christmas cards from me.

I used to send out a hundred Christmas cards, all with hand-written notes inside. That number has since dwindled to around sixty. A few close friends died. A few close friends turned into enemies. A few close friends kept sending me the card with the wolf kissing the caribou. Here are a few guiding principles for Christmas card giving that I have developed over the years:

1. Before sending out photos of your kids, make sure that they are not gap-toothed idiots. They so often are. To avoid embarrassing yourself, stick with the baby Jesus, the Infant of Prague, Frosty the Snowman, or Santa's helpful little elves. If it ain't broke, don't fix it. Frosty ain't broke.

2. Do not send a Christmas card from South Beach, Puerto

Vallarta, or Tahiti. Christmas is supposed to conjure up images of biblical lands where miracles occur. Or images of the North Pole. South Beach is not biblical. Tahiti is not arctic. Puerto Vallarta is just plain wrong.

3. Do not send a Christmas *postcard.* Do not send a Christmas greeting on Christmas *notepaper.* Send a proper Christmas card or send nothing. As Oscar Wilde once put it, "In matters of great importance, style, not sincerity, is the vital thing."

4. Do not send a Christmas card telling everyone how much you are enjoying the golf in South Carolina or the tennis in Maui. It inspires an emotion called *Schadenjoiedefreude,* the rapturous joy one experiences when somebody crows about enjoying an activity that would make you retch. Seeing Andrea Bocelli. Hearing Andrea Bocelli. Attending Burning Man. Playing the hammered dulcimer. Playing the hammered dulcimer at Burning Man with Andrea Bocelli.

5. If you are going to send a card with a doggie dressed up in a Santa cap, do not send it two years in a row. Or three. Or every year for the last decade. It isn't just me. People keep track of this sort of thing.

6. Do not send a one-size-fits-all Christmas letter informing us that your wife recently appeared in an amateur production of *The Pajama Game* in Tuscany. Just the thought of senior citizens cavorting onstage in Tuscan pajamas is enough to make one ill.

7. Do not tell mes that you recently went hiking in Wales. I don't see how that sort of information can improve my mood, or anyone else's.

8. If you are going to send a Christmas letter, do not tell me how devastated you are that your budgerigar died. This is not the kind of information you should share with everyone. It is deeply, deeply personal.

9. If you include names like Jared, Lourdes, Brooklyn, or Justice in your Christmas mailing, please remind us whether

they are children or pets. It's increasingly difficult to keep track these days.

10. Do not send a Christmas card where Frosty looks forlorn. Sad, yes. Crestfallen, fine. But not forlorn.

Am I making too much of this? Yes, of course I am making too much of this; I make too much of everything. But the reason I make too much of everything is because everyone else makes too little of anything. Everyone else sends out Christmas cards without thinking through the ramifications. Too many people just go through the motions.

My three favorite Christmas cards were all addressed to Santa at the North Pole. I got them in December 1982 at the General Post Office on Eighth Avenue in New York, which served as a collection point for all the letters to Santa written by children in New York City. Johnny Carson used to read a selection of these cards out loud on the *Tonight Show* and encourage viewers to stop by the post office, pick up a few of these cards, and buy toys for the little kids who had sent them. I picked out three. On Christmas morning, my wife and I delivered one Donkey Kong game to a kid on the Lower East Side and another one to a kid living in a housing project in the twenties. Then we went to a homeless shelter in the East Village to deliver a Walkman to a little boy who had written his letter in French.

There was, we were told, no little French boy in the shelter. But then someone spoke up and said that there was a Danish man with multiple personalities in the shelter, one of whom was a twelve-year-old Haitian boy. New York was great in the Eighties. We left the Walkman and walked home. We were feeling very, very good. We did not eat that day. We fasted.

One year later, on Christmas morning, our daughter was born. People born on Christmas Day tend to hate it, because they get jobbed out of gifts and parties and because nobody calls to wish them a happy birthday. But if you are the parent of a child born on Christmas Day, you will always feel special. You will feel that it is a sign from God, even if you don't believe in God. A Christmas baby is the best gift you will ever get. It doesn't matter how it got here.

This is probably why I hang on to so many of those old Christmas cards. Many of these cards depict Joseph and Mary in the stable in Bethlehem with the baby Jesus, the Light of the World, swaddled in a manger. For Joseph and Mary, there could not be a better Christmas present than their newborn child.

I know the feeling.

CHAPTER 4

Jingle Bell Rock

*Taking the Christ
Out of Christmas Songs*

Andrew Ferguson

IN THE CITY where I live, one of the pop music radio stations shifts to an all-Christmas music format beginning in . . . oh, I don't know, late August?

Kidding! No, I think the transition takes place a couple weeks before Thanksgiving, which gives us all plenty of time to get sick of our seasonal favorites long before the season officially begins. The all-Christmas programming used to start Thanksgiving week. And before that, many years ago, it began the weekend *after* Thanksgiving. This is in keeping with the familiar chronological acceleration that nowadays places the tubby rubber Santas up against the plastic jack-o'-lanterns on the shelves at the local CVS, right next to the back-to-school supplies, which will soon be replaced by Valentine candy.

I dislike the acceleration of Christmas as much as anyone else, but with no access to a Pandora account and lacking satellite radio in my car, I listen to the station all the same, until I can't stand it anymore. Like the season itself, my moment of Christmas-music overfeeding arrives earlier and earlier with each passing year. In a few years I will be driving around shouting for the death of the entire Mormon Tabernacle Choir before Columbus Day.

But I am captive to the station's programming long enough

to notice a few things. Chief among them is that during the modern Christmas season you can't get away from Mariah Carey. Even now, many years after the salad days of her career began to wilt, she's like our generation's Queen of Christmas—or the new Mrs. Claus. Or the Transitioning Santa. She's everywhere.

Her status rests on the song "All I Want for Christmas Is You," released twenty-one years ago as of this writing and perhaps the only Christmas song written in the last forty years to show the staying power of a standard, like "Have Yourself a Merry Little Christmas" or "The Christmas Song." Mariah Carey wrote "All I Want" with a collaborator. He arranged it, produced it, and, through the miracle of digital programming, played all the instruments. But it is Mariah who filled the crucial role, not as singer but as Yuletide sex kitten: She appeared in a music video that has become a feature of the season almost as indelible as the song itself. In it she is seen disporting—I'm sorry, there's no other word for it—along winter landscapes in a snug-fitting snowsuit and then donning a Santa's cap and red velvet mini-skirt and crossing her legs enthusiastically in the ample lap of Santa himself. He looks extremely jolly, and why not?

"Make my wish come true," she sings, in the emphatic tones of an oil barge lost in a fog bank. "All I want for Christmas is you, baby." I can listen to the song more often than most of the songs our all-Christmas radio station plays—roughly twice as often, for example, as I can listen to Bon Jovi singing "Backdoor Santa." It's a catchy rave-up with an impressive rhythm section, even when you know the tom toms and snappy snare are really just the electronic pulsations of a drum machine. And while it's more successful than most Christmas songs of its time, it is representative of them, too. Mostly in this: It doesn't have anything to do with Christmas.

By design, according to Mariah Carey's cowriter, "All I Want" is a bit of musical misdirection, a love song swaddled in Christmas clothes (velvet miniskirt, Santa cap). The seasonal references to reindeer and snow and Santa and Christmas trees are used as a means to convey the singer's earthier, and less Christmassy, need for a hunk-a hunk-a burning love. At first glance, of course, this is a much more marketable yearning than the yearning Christmas is supposed to give rise to. It could be worse. I think of a version of "O Holy Night" released a decade ago by one of Mariah Carey's early imitators, Christina Aguilera. Her recording of this old and explicitly Christian hymn was probably intended as an assertion of piety, but it might be the biggest blow to the Christian religion since the Turks overran the Byzantines at the Battle of Manzikert in 1071.

To convey her depth of religious feeling, Christina borrows her mentor's signature vocal trick, using several notes to sing a single syllable. Musicologists call it melisma. It is an old technique, common to Gregorian chants from long ago, but it's more familiar to contemporary audiences through the vein-popping exertions of the late Whitney Houston and countless singers who have kneecapped our national anthem before televised sporting events. As the singer slides around in search of the note to match the syllable, melisma can sound to the amateur ear—mine anyway—like someone handed a pennywhistle to a meth-head.

So it is with Christina Aguilera when she opens fire at "O Holy Night." The problem with melisma, at least as it's done now, is that it draws attention to the singer and away from the song, an effect that is especially crippling in Christmas music, which is, according to tradition anyway, supposed to be about something other than self. I know nothing of her religious convictions, but Christina Aguilera certainly sounds sincere, or enthusiastic at least. She takes some of her syllables—the "lee-ee-ee-ee" in "holy," for instance—on a roller-coaster ride of nine or ten quarter notes until her voice flies off the rails and goes crashing down on the next syllable: "na-ah–ah–ah–ttttt!" For the last twelve bars a gospel piano vamps behind her as she scats on "Jee-jeee-jeeeee-zuz . . . oh! . . . Jeeezzzussss uh-Churist . . ." You can't tell whether she wants to praise Him or date Him.

When it comes to Christmas, then, Mariah Carey and the other melisma mamas might be right to leave Jesus out of it altogether and settle instead into Santa's lap for three minutes of forelock tugging. Most singers and songwriters do the same, avoiding piety in favor of a frolic. This is the common course contemporary Christmas music has traveled over the last several decades. The most prominent trend has been toward what the music industry calls the "novelty song"—a ditty so insubstantial that it wobbles from funny to infuriating in thirty-two bars. Excellent examples of novelties in the secular songbook are "How Much Is That Doggy in the Window?" and "Disco Duck" from ye olden times on up to the more recent "Rock Me Amadeus" and "Crazy Frog." And so my all-Christmas station sputters with "The Chipmunk Song," "Grandma Got Run Over by a Reindeer," "Here Comes Santa Claus," and "I Saw Mommy Kissing Santa Claus." If Weird Al Yankovic suddenly converted and took responsibility for writing all our new Christmas songs, he could do no worse than "Be Claus I Got High," "Boob Job for Christmas," or "Daddy Please (Don't Get Drunk This Christmas)."

In a way, these are simply successors to such non-Christmas Christmas classics as "Jingle Bells," "Silver Bells," "Let It Snow," and "Frosty the Snowman"—songs that, respectively, are about antique modes of transportation, seasonal decorations in a department store, the weather, and the creepy resuscitation of inanimate objects. The closest we get to the source of the holiday are Christmas songs that celebrate the celebration of Christmas, which is to say: Songs that are at least two removes from the actual event. "The Christmas Waltz" tells us "it's that time of year when the world falls in love," but why does the world fall in love? We are told to have ourselves a merry little Christmas, but the song doesn't tell us why our Christmas, big or little, is supposed to be merry. And what's the significance of a winter wonderland, besides the new bird replacing the blue bird?

We live in a secular age, a post-Christian age. We attend "winter festivals," throw "holiday parties," use "season's greetings" as the all-purpose salutation. Our public schools, our government, and our retail outlets have purged Christmas of its religious meaning. Why not purge our Christmas music, too? But I think something else is going on as well. If we insist that we treat this religious holiday exclusively with a secular levity, through rock-and-roll come-ons and joke songs, we might get the impression that we can't use levity to treat religious matters. If singers and musicians think they can be jolly only by de-Christianizing Christmas, then we might begin to believe that the only way to appreciate its true significance is to sound as miserable as Christina Aguilera in full melisma mode. We might even begin to believe that fun (pleasure, delight, enjoyment of the wonders of the world) is the opposite of religion. And come to think of it, most people already do believe this. Especially Christians.

It's an old problem, of course—an old problem even for Christmas music. In the early church, Christmas replaced the baptism of Jesus as the preeminent celebration of the season because it stood as a happy rebuke to the Manicheans. Believing as they did in the absolute division of spirit and matter, no group of heretics has ever been gloomier. The celebration of Christmas was a way of telling the world: This really happened, to a real mother and a real child, made in flesh and blood, the coming together of God and man. And music itself is the natural expression of the union of spirit and matter, the physical act of plucking strings or hammering keys or thrumming vocal cords to produce something that points beyond the physical. Unless you use a drum machine.

No other holiday is so intimately connected to music, so quickly evoked by a simple melody or even mere sounds—sleigh bells or the immense whispering of snowfall at night. The idea of Christmas as a musical celebration finally took hold when peasants and other lowly folk began adapting local dance tunes to the purpose. The origins of Christmas music in dance music is worth remembering. The tunes, outfitted with words of praise and the appropriate narratives of Jesus and Mary and Joseph, of the Three Kings and the shepherds, were an effusion of popular piety—and a rebellion against the grim impositions of church hierarchy throughout Germany and, later, England. A good carol, said the great musicologist Percy Deamer, "was witness to the spirit of a more spontaneous and undoubting faith." The effusions were organic, growing from the bottom up, and like the Gospels themselves, filled with metaphors taken from field and hearth:

> The tree of life my soul hath seen
> Laden with fruit and always green
> The trees of nature fruitless be
> Compared with Christ the apple tree.

Deamer traced the word "carol" back through old French to the Greek word for "an encircling dance." Movement and dynamism and joy were the essential attributes, inseparable from the religious meaning. The message of Christmas was the Christian message, too: the Light coming into the world and the darkness proving powerless against it. What's not to celebrate? Why not dance?

"To take life"—and hence Christmas—"with real seriousness is to take it joyfully," Deamer went on. "For seriousness is only sad when it is superficial: the carol is thus nearer to the truth because it is jolly." The opposite isn't necessarily true, by the way. "All I Want for Christmas Is You" might be described as jolly; no one would describe it as serious. "Joy to the World," on the other hand, is both. A Christmas carol is meant to liberate us from phony seriousness and phony good cheer.

In the past that lesson has often been lost, at times even more thoroughly than in our own day—a reminder that should cheer us up, if you'll forgive the expression. The serious joy, or the joyful seriousness, of Christmas is offensive to the grim Christian. When Oliver Cromwell's Puritans seized power from a pious English king, one of their first official acts was to ban Christmas observances of any kind. A pamphleteering divine named Hezekiah Woodward explained the reasoning.

Christmas Day, he wrote, is "the old Heathen's Feasting Day, in honor of Saturn their Idol God, the Papist's Massing Day, the Profane Man's Ranting Day, the Superstitious Man's Idol Day, the Multitude's Idle Day, Satan's Working Day, the True Christian Man's Fasting Day." With all that competition, the best option for a "True Christian Man" was to hunker down on Christmas Eve, foreswear meat and drink, and wait for December 26. Singing—particularly singing songs of joy—was out of the question. "We are persuaded, no one thing more hinderest the Gospel work all the yearlong, than doth the observation of that Idol Day once in a year." Imagine what they would have done with Mariah Carey!

"Yule tide is fool tide," went the Puritans' dismissive slogan (which was truer than the Puritans knew, probably, if you give "fool" the meaning St. Paul gave it when he told us to be "fools for Christ's sake"). And once in a while, at Christmas, buried in tinsel and credit card receipts, a practicing Christian might be tempted to agree. It's a familiar human paradox that the phony good cheer of secular Christmas increases even as the genuine joy of Christmas recedes; the music of the holiday grows more insistent and frenetic even as it moves further away from its origin in true delight. The question is why a secular culture bothers to write and sing and play Christmas music at all.

G. K. Chesterton wondered the same thing. How does music sprung from the loam of Christian observance survive the banalities of the post-Christian age? One answer—Chesterton's answer—is that we don't live in a post-Christian age after all, not really. More to the point, it's impossible to live in a post-Christian age. Some things can't be undone, and chief among them is the Light that was lit the first Christmas morning, while choirs of angels sang above. It can be ridiculed and parodied, satirized and scoffed at, obscured and sentimentalized, but it won't be extinguished. So even a secular age continues to go through the motions, singing the same songs, sometimes the old songs, without quite knowing why.

"The great majority," Chesterton wrote, "will go on observing forms that cannot be explained; they will keep Christmas with Christmas gifts and Christmas benedictions; they will continue to do it; and suddenly one day they will wake up and discover why."

Who knows when or how? But every now and then an image pops to mind when I listen to my all-Christmas radio station. I like to think of a sophisticated fellow, impatient with religion and educated in the contemporary manner, walking, let's say, past a church in a December twilight, maybe musing about Mariah's snowsuit or wondering how Grandma got run over, and then perhaps he will linger for a moment and sneak a peek at the manger scene, throw a glance into the crib, and hear the strains of the carol from within: "Mild, He lays His glory by, born that man no more may die." And suddenly he will wake up and discover why.

"Wait a minute!" he will say. "All I want for Christmas is *You!*"

CHAPTER 5

Oh, Tannenbaum

A Tradition Unlike Any Other

Christopher Caldwell

I LAST THOUGHT seriously about the meaning of Christmas trees late one December Saturday a quarter-century ago. Dusk was falling, flurries were flying, and it was cold. I was dragging a Fraser fir tree down the breakdown lane of the McGrath and O'Brien Highway in Somerville, Massachusetts, midway through a two-mile trek from a Christmas tree lot to my third-floor apartment. The tree was gigantic. It was about nine feet tall, two feet taller than the room I planned to put it in. Half an hour into my walk it occurred to me that holding the tree by the tip and dragging the base of it along the asphalt might be damaging it, scuffing it up so it wouldn't sit properly in the Christmas-tree stand. I dropped the tree for a sec and looked. Yikes! Abrasion had beveled the foot of it, so it was shaped like a chisel, and had taken out the bottom tier of branches, too. But I didn't have to worry about fitting my tree in the Christmas tree stand, I reflected, because I didn't *have* a Christmas tree stand. I had no ornaments or lights for my new tree, either. I was not good at planning in those days.

"Poor planning," if we may euphemize, is how I wound up where I was that evening. My life was like a country-western song. I was young and married, soon to be young and unmarried. I couldn't even keep track of things that were of desperate importance to me, like the hour the liquor store closed every evening. My quondam wife seemed to be avoiding the apartment I was living in. But it was not out of the question she would drop by. If she did, our young daughter might be with her. So I had resolved that, come what may, there would be a Christmas tree in the apartment. How to arrange this was tricky. I did not own a car. None of my car-owning friends would have understood why my apartment, which never had milk, bread, eggs, or clean clothes in it, now needed a conifer. So I made the long walk from Winter Hill to a swampy parking lot where I knew there was a Christmas tree seller, out where the highway crossed the Mystic River.

My daughter didn't come back. I never got a tree stand. The tree itself leaned in the corner of my living room for the whole of the holiday season. But I was glad it was there. It felt right, and it brought me a minor kind of joy, which was the kind of joy I specialized in at the time. I had, it seemed, a thing about Christmas trees.

But so do most people. The Christmas tree has escaped every earnest attack on Christmas and every cynical attempt to run the holiday down. Unlike Christmas pageants, Christmas office parties, Christmas TV specials, and virtually everything that happens between Thanksgiving dessert and Midnight Mass, the Christmas tree has no detractors. It is venerated in all its forms (at least all its natural ones), from the big, bright-lit firs on the White House lawn to the dandelion-sized bonsais sitting on tabletops in studio apartments. The ballroom-filling behemoth in the classic children's book *Mr. Willowby's Christmas Tree* embodies the grandeur of the holiday. But so, too, in its way, does the bare drooping pine, too weak even to support a single Christmas ornament, needleless but far from needless, on the *Charlie Brown Christmas* special.

How the Christmas tree came to enjoy its almost unanimous prestige has been the subject of much speculation. Pagan and Christian currents both flow into the way we celebrate the winter birth of Jesus, and vegetation is involved in almost all of them. The Druids venerated mistletoe. The Romans put up trees at Kalends, at the beginning of each month. Poinsettias were first brought back by the U.S. ambassador to Mexico, and later secretary of war, Joel Poinsett, who used them to brighten his South Carolina home in the winter months.

In England, Glastonbury Cathedral claimed to have received the rod of St. Joseph of Arimathea, the "good and just" disciple who took Jesus' body down from the cross "and wrapped it in linen, and laid it in a sepulcher that was hewn in stone, wherein never man before was laid." It was said that Joseph stuck this rod into dirt in the Glastonbury churchyard, and that it miraculously turned into a thorn bush that blossomed every Christmas. In 1752, when the British authorities dropped eleven days from the year in order to make the transition from the Julian to the Gregorian calendar, thousands of Christians showed up at Glastonbury on Christmas to ensure the bush would blossom. It didn't. Protestant Britain had held out from adopting the more rational Gregorian arrangement in the first place because it had been favored by Europe's Catholic powers. So when the bush failed to bloom, many took it as evidence that the new calendar was not just inconvenient but heretical.

My grandparents were a bit like those Glastonbury vigil keepers. They would buy their Christmas tree late on the afternoon of December 24 and spend the rest of the evening trimming it. This is in line with the old Anglo-Saxon tradition of getting a Yule log to burn in the hearth the night before Christmas, a tradition that died out sometime in the nineteenth century. My grandparents never said why they bought the tree so late. Procrastination is as likely an explanation as tradition. They would keep it up for the whole twelve days of Christmas (appropriately enough, since the Twelfth Day, or Epiphany, is an older celebration than Christmas itself). Then they would throw the tree onto the snowbound porch and vacuum all the dried-up needles off the living room carpet, so that, for the rest of the year, whenever my grandmother vacuumed, even to prepare for a Fourth of July cocktail party, the hot Electrolux would fill the house with a powerful, piney, Christmassy aroma.

My father loved his parents' Christmas traditions, and, really, decorating the tree on Christmas Eve makes a great deal of romantic, atmospheric, sensation-heightening sense. It means that on Christmas morning, you wake up to the sight of your tree for the first time. But getting a tree late in the season cuts against the modern American acquisitive spirit. It reduces the quantity of Christmas-tree-enjoyment hours. My sisters and I had been whipped into a frenzy of "Christmas spirit" by various gimme-gimme-gimme television product ads, and our pleading to get the season underway began with the first session of Saturday morning cartoons after Thanksgiving. My father could not stand up to it. The result was a compromise under which we got the tree a week or two before Christmas.

What everyone most loves about Christmas trees—the sense of bringing a forest into one's house, the standing it up, the gaudy garlanding of it—is the contribution of America's largest ethnic group, the Germans. "That childish, open-hearted simplicity," wrote one of the correspondents of the English folklorist Clement Miles in his 1912 history of Christmas ritual and tradition, "makes Christmas essentially German. The German is himself simple, warm-hearted, unpretentious with something at the bottom of him which is childlike in the best sense." (One assumes the opinion was revised in Miles' 1914 edition.) This German tradition passed to the United States before the mid-nineteenth-century wave of German immigration, but only just before, around the time of the coronation of Britain's first German queen, Victoria.

Much aided by the enthusiastic decorating of Princess Helena of Mecklenburg, the tree craze proliferated among upper-crust households in France and England and, after that, in America. Christmas trees were signals of one's cosmopolitanism, on the one hand, and a lot of fun on the other. So they spread in rather the way the American Halloween tradition of trick-or-treat has spread in continental Europe since the turn of this century. The roots of our style of Christmas decoration lie in the Alsatian city of Strasbourg and date from the seventeenth century. The American folklorist George William Douglas had described the original tradition as one in which, on New Year's Eve, Alsatian women would set up a fir tree next to a fountain, bedecking it "with ribbons, eggshells, and little figures," representing shepherds and various butts of humor.

Even in the 1970s, certain German tree-trimming traditions lived on, and live on still. Germans are said to favor draping the boughs of their firs with shiny, foot-long metallic threads of *Engelshaar*, or angel hair. This is what we now call "tinsel." My childhood coincided with the golden age of tinsel, because American manufacturers, in the wake of World War II, had learned that you could mass-produce it cheaply, out of thin little strips of lead. There was nothing gossamer, angelic, or fairylike about this stuff. The Ornament Industrial Complex renamed it "icicles." Did it hang plumb, as icicles do? Did it ever! It took only a few strands of this leaden tinsel to make a bough, once upward-pointed, sag under the weight. Once we'd applied a few boxes' worth to our tree, it looked like something made of chrome, or maybe one of the *Apollo* lunar modules, with the baubles poking out of it like headlights. Alas, around 1970, a federal ban on certain uses of lead put an end to "icicles," so we had to substitute the child-safe polyurethane version of tinsel, which didn't taste nearly as good as the lead kind.

Already in my childhood, there was a class war ongoing over whether one ought to light one's tree with big bulbs in many colors or little sparkly white ones. The former were more festive, the latter more sophisticated. We were a festive family. In the years before Arab oil embargoes, my parents would drive us through the French Canadian neighborhoods in nearby mill towns, where those primary-colored cone-shaped bulbs were strung along every porch railing, and floodlit Santas, homemade crèches, and glow-in-the-dark plastic snowmen crowded the front lawns—stuff that was visible, but not in quite such profusion, in the slightly tonier neighborhood they had moved the family into.

Writing a century ago, Miles, the Germanophile English folklorist mentioned above, noted that "in Germany the Christmas-tree is not a luxury for well-to-do people as in England, but a necessity." Outside of its German place of origin, celebrating Christmas properly meant considerable effort and expenditure. In America as in England, Christmas festivities early on became a badge of status. University of Massachusetts historian Stephen Nissenbaum noted in his 1996 study *The Battle for Christmas* that the first American Christmas tree fad found its most ardent promoters in a wealthy and sophisticated vanguard—people you might describe as the "limousine liberals" or the "cultural elite" of their time. Many who put up the first Christmas trees were adherents of Unitarianism, a liberal wing of New England Congregationalism that was then emerging, under the leadership of such preachers as William Ellery Channing and (briefly) Ralph Waldo Emerson, as a faith in its own right. These people were skeptical of older traditions, not excluding Christianity itself.

Nissenbaum shows that Unitarians, a century before anyone had ever heard of shopping malls or Saturday morning television ads, were troubled by American materialism. They were also among the most enthusiastic fans of the child-rearing philosophy of Johann Heinrich Pestalozzi, a sort of Swiss Dr. Spock, who had gained a worldwide following. In the 1820s, Pestalozzi was assailing what he saw as the traditional Christian moral teaching that "willfulness" was a danger to children's souls. Since a child's will could only impede the working of divine grace, the old theory held, the best thing a parent could do was *break* it. Pestalozzi thought this was wrong. The will needed not to be broken, but to be trained. In fact, uncorrupted children probably had more reliable wills than adults, and could serve as role models; adults might do well to imitate their innocent joy. Pestalozzi's disciples saw modern Christmases as a way to use various emotional triggers to fill the house with the joy of childhood. Surprise was important (as joy's occasion and inducement). So was the mystery of the gift-giver Santa Claus (to keep children from trying to manipulate the real gift-givers, the parents, thereby tainting the innocence of that joy). So were Christmas trees (as joy's magical backdrop).

The typical American Christmas, then, was the invention of secularizing cultural elites. But the yeoman culture of the country was too strong to let it remain exclusive. The snob appeal of Christmas was undermined by the pious people who cared most fervently about it. "Much of the emphasis on profound worship that now shows itself in the American Christmas owes its vigor not to the mainstream English stock but to later immigrants," wrote University of Pennsylvania professor Tristram P. Coffin in his *Book of Christmas Folklore* in 1973. "With their pyramids of candles, their crèches, poinsettias, and *tannenbaums*, they have brought back into the commemoration a wonder that had almost disappeared." Today's Christmas is the result. It has elements of both a high-class holiday (from the *Nutcracker Suite* to the Dickensian craft fair) and a low-class holiday (from

"Grandma Got Run Over by a Reindeer" to the Black Friday "Door-Buster" sales at shopping malls).

A Christmas tree, in particular, combines two seemingly irreconcilable things. It is one of the last repositories of nineteenth-century high culture in common use, but it is also democratic, approachable, and subsumed in love of one's fellow man. This makes a Christmas tree a thing of joy to everyone. It is worth going out on a snowy day to get one, even if you are not sure you will have anyone to share it with.

I remember arriving with my nine-foot tree at the front door of the triple-decker I lived in twenty-five years ago. My shoulders were knotted with pain. I was so exhausted it didn't occur to me that in order to get that thing up the stairway to the third floor, I ought to pick it up. Instead I dragged it, with the branches catching on the railings and the trunk hammering on the stairs. Open swung the door of the second-floor apartment, the apartment occupied by my Albanian landlady, with whom I had never exchanged a friendly word. I spoke to her only on the first day of every month, when she would hammer on my door at seven in the morning yelling, "Renty! Renty!" and late on certain nights—it was impossible to predict which ones— when she would respond to my clattering progress up the stairs by opening her door and saying, "What is it now?"

That evening she lurched, muttering, into the hallway, glared at me for a moment the way she always did, and then looked past me to the big fir I was struggling with. "Oh," she said coldly. "Merry Christmas." Then she shut the door and went back inside.

CHAPTER 6

The Nativity Stories

The Best (and Worst) Christmas Movies Ever

Sonny Bunch

WHAT'S THE GREATEST Christmas movie of all time? Well, before we tackle that question, we have to take a step back and ask what makes a movie a "Christmas movie" in the first place. It's a trickier problem than you think. Being set during the Christmas season is a necessary, but not sufficient, factor. If all you needed were jingle bells in the background, then Shane Black—the brains behind *Lethal Weapon, Kiss Kiss Bang Bang*, and *Iron Man 3*, all of which take place around Christmastime— would be the undisputed champ of Christmas cinema, the auteur of Noel. But none of those movies are really *Christmas* movies. So he's not.

What about *Die Hard*, the 1988 Bruce Willis action classic? It was released during summer blockbuster season, but it's about terrorists who take over an office building during a Christmas party. So many film-school hipsters have declared it a Christmas movie that BuzzFeed—BuzzFeed!—felt the need to publish a piece declaring that the take was no longer hot. But *Die Hard* is clearly *not* a Christmas movie, because Christmas isn't intrinsic to the plot. The story could have just as easily taken place during, say, the Fourth of July. All that matters to the mechanics of *Die Hard* is that people gather at Nakatomi Plaza so Alan Rickman can become an international star by lecturing his hostages on the finer points of bespoke menswear.

In order to make the cut as a Christmas movie, the holiday has to be integral to a film's actions and inform its themes. Take *Home Alone*, Chris Columbus' 1990 film about a kid named Kevin whose family goes on vacation without him. The plot involves a pair of criminals robbing homes that are (a) filled with new loot, in the form of Christmas presents, and (b) empty of people, who are traveling for the holidays. Throw in the fact that the movie's key themes are family togetherness and forgiveness, and the taxonomy is settled: *Home Alone* is definitely a Christmas movie.

Is it a *great* Christmas movie, though? Probably not: As Barack Obama said of Hillary Clinton, it's likable enough. Screenwriter John Hughes deftly mixed sentimentality and comedy, popping a heartwarming conclusion on top of what is basically just a bawdy amalgamation of body humor and annoying kid stuff. *Home Alone* isn't as funny as the funniest Christmas movies, and yet its sentimentality is more cloying than even the schmaltziest ones.

❄️

But at least we're getting somewhere now. As with *Home Alone*, the great Christmas movies tend to meld sentimentality with humor. Yet we generally classify them under one phylum or the other. And when it comes to the sentimental species—the ones that make you well up, even though you know everything works out in the end and even though you've seen the movie a hundred times—there are only a couple of legitimate choices for GOAT (that's greatest of all time, for you noobs).

The grandfather of the genre is *Miracle on 34th Street*. The 1947 classic from George Seaton is about proving that Santa Claus, the Christmassiest figure of them all in our increasingly secular society, is real. The story of a doubtful little girl whose harridan of a working mother has driven all faith from her, *Mir-*

acle on 34th Street is about reclaiming wonder from cynicism and the importance of opening yourself up to love. It also might be the greatest endorsement of the U.S. Postal Service ever, with the film's climactic scene revolving around giant bags of mail being delivered to the courtroom. (It's amusing that in a seventy-year-old movie, the biggest anachronism is an ironclad belief in the competence of the Post Office.)

But the king of this category is Frank Capra's *It's a Wonderful Life*, the 1946 monument to Americana. Capra embraces a sort of communal individualism that has long been the bedrock of American society: Jimmy Stewart's George Bailey is a hero who saves his brother and the town pharmacist and the family bank through a combination of blind bravery and devoted selflessness.

Mind you, when you look at it in a certain light, this neighborliness can edge a bit close to socialism. And truth be told, Potterville gets kind of a bad rap. Oh, sure, it's filled with gambling parlors and cheap floozies. But on the other hand, think of all the gambling parlors and cheap floozies! Isn't that what makes America great?

Still, show me a man who doesn't get choked up when we flash back to Bedford Falls where George and his family are surrounded by the singing townsfolk who've just bailed him out, and I'll show you a callous monster unfit for human society. *It's a Wonderful Life* is a Christmas classic in spite of—or, heaven help us, maybe even because of—its commie sympathies.

You would think that *A Christmas Carol* should fall into this category of greats, too, but the problem with Dickens' classic is that there are so many competing movie versions to choose from. The best-loved straight-up adaptation is probably 1951's *Scrooge*, starring Alastair Sim as the titular miser. Then again, some people prefer the classic 1938 version starring Reginald Owen. And who can forget the 1970 musical adaptation starring Albert Finney? Or the 1984 version starring George C.

Scott? Or the 1999 TV movie starring Jean-Luc Picard? Or the 2009 motion-capture version directed by Robert Zemeckis and starring Jim Carrey as not only Scrooge but also the ghosts of Christmas Past, Present, and Future, too? (Actually, you can forget about that one. Not only is it distressingly terrible as a dramatic execution, but the motion-capture animation used by Zemeckis sits in the same Uncanny Valley in which his previous Christmas film, *The Polar Express*, was trapped. Instead of feeling sympathy for Tiny Tim, you get a subconscious feeling of revulsion. Because he looks like a cartoon replicant.)

In truth, I'm not terribly fond of any of them. Yet Dickens' book is usefully Shakespearean in that its bones and its structure and its very language have been used for all sorts of adaptations. Many, perhaps most, of these are dreadful (*An American Carol*, *Ghosts of Girlfriends Past*), but every once in a while you get a classic. My personal favorite is Bill Murray's *Scrooged*, which doubles as a fantastic Christmas movie and the best commentary on the soullessness of the television industry and the craven executives who have run it since *Network*.

Scrooged manages to rejigger *A Christmas Carol* in ways that are, at times, heartwarming. The adventure of Frank (Murray) with the Ghost of Christmas Past can get the waterworks going: When we see how he lost Karen Black and how much his mother loves him, it is, as the Ghost says, "Niagara Falls, Frankie Angel." The tears, they burn! Fortunately for people who are emotionally dead inside (like me) there aren't too many of these moments, and *Scrooged* is deeply, darkly hilarious. The reimagining of Jacob Marley as a golfing, worm-ridden Lee Iacocca type is sublime, while Bobcat Goldthwait's laid-off, warbling, shotgun-wielding, drink-sodden cubicle monkey adds the perfect dash of realistic absurdity. In one of those strange tricks of literally alchemy, *Scrooged* takes sentimental source material and turns it into a movie that's not just a comedy, but a great one.

Many of the Christmas comedies since the early 1980s have lived in a dark place. Before *Scrooged* came *Gremlins*, a comedy/thriller about a group of tiny monsters that takes over a small town after a young man fails to follow the rules of caring for them. You might not think of *Gremlins* as a Christmas movie, but remember: Not only does it take place during Christmas, but a key portion of the film involves the protagonist's girlfriend coming to grips with the death of her father years before. While he was dressed as Santa. And trying to climb down a chimney.

Dark in a different way is Tim Burton's *The Nightmare before Christmas*, the only movie that works for both Christmas *and* Halloween. It features great set design and a fascinating premise paired with catchy tunes. Stop-motion animation has nothing on the more traditional variety, however, and there's a reason Boris Karloff's *How the Grinch Stole Christmas!* has been in constant rotation for the last five decades.

But *The Grinch* gets downgraded in my book for inspiring what has to be the single *worst* Christmas movie in history: Jim Carrey's live-action adaptation of the same name. It's pretty remarkable that Carrey has managed to star in not one, but two, of the most unnecessary adaptations of beloved Christmas movies. If you want someone to crap all over a Christmas classic, Carrey's your guy. And you might want to look out: Given that his Grinch came out in 2000 and his Scrooge dropped in 2009, we're just about due for Another Garbage Jim Carrey Christmas Movie.

As far as the animated division goes in our little field taxonomy, for my money it's topped by *A Charlie Brown Christmas*. Who can forget the dinky little Christmas tree bowed over at the top? The 1965 classic also does something very few Christmas movies then, or now, would dare to: It features a recitation from the Bible and a reminder of what the day is really all about.

Given that December 25 now rivals the Fourth of July weekend as a marquee release date, I guess it's not surprising that so few Christmas movies are religious in nature. If you're trying to cram people into 3D IMAX cathedrals with laser-aligned sound and convince them that popcorn and Diet Coke are worthy substitutes for the body and blood of Christ, you probably don't want to remind them of the fact that they're ducking out on paying respects to the guy who died for their sins. The only Christmas movie I can think of in recent years with an explicitly churchy message is 2006's *The Nativity Story*. It also happens to be the only film to have debuted at the Vatican rather than Mann's Chinese.

All of which is to say that Santa has more or less replaced Jesus as the cinematic face of the season. So you would think he'd be treated with a little more respect. The aforementioned *Miracle on 34th Street* notwithstanding, Santa is more frequently blasphemed against than venerated these days. Do you have any idea how many cheap, terrible, horror Christmas movies there are? Among (many) others, there's *Silent Night, Deadly Night* (1984), *Santa's Slay* (2005), and *Santa Claws* (1996). If I'm forced to pick a "favorite," I guess I go with *Santa's Slay*; not only is the pun to die for (*get it?*), it also stars former professional wrestler Bill Goldberg as a demon Mr. Claus.

It's one thing to portray Ol' Saint Nick as a demonic murderer; that's all in good fun. But none of those movies is as blasphemous as 2003's *Bad Santa*. Billy Bob Thornton stars as a safe-cracking drunk whose holiday routine is to take a job as a department store Santa in order to infiltrate high-end shopping malls and make off with a sack full of goodies on Christmas Eve. Yet even a movie like this—which delights in shocking audiences with Thornton's crook dressed up as Santa and performing all manner of mayhem—winds up being transformed by the idea of Christmas. In time, Thornton's lecherous, conniving character learns to care for others and himself.

It's deeply funny and, in its own perverse way, deeply sweet. Even though it's played for shock value, the truth is the movie wouldn't work without Christmas in it. Improbably, it's become a cable Christmas classic. But it's not *the* cable Christmas classic.

In 1997 TNT began running one movie, over and over, for twenty-four consecutive hours spanning Christmas Eve and Christmas Day. This movie has earned a place in our culture, in our hearts, and in our homes as a mainstay of the Christmas season. I speak, of course, of *A Christmas Story*.

The 1983 film did solid, if unremarkable, business in its initial theatrical run. But the quest of a towheaded scamp named Ralphie to get a Red Ryder BB gun for Christmas resonated with people over the long haul. In part, this is because Ralphie manages to navigate the everyday childhood indignities most of us remember with, if not fondness, then some sentimentality: the taste of soap after ill-advised wise-acreage; the ever-looming threat of bullies on the prowl; the overwhelming, soulful desire to own a piece of exquisite, manly hardware frustrated—over and over.

The movie's enduring popularity speaks to memoirist and screenwriter Jean Shepherd's ability to capture a sort of idealized American Christmas, putting a humorous gloss on all the secular accouterments of the season. Who doesn't remember taking a trip to some shady lot filled with hucksters looking to pawn off thinned-out, half-brown pine trees? Or counting down the days until the home-cooked Christmas goose (or ham or roast) is ready to eat? Or putting on a ridiculous piece of clothing sent by a loved one, snapping a photo of yourself in the getup, and then burying it in a closet, never to be seen again? And lurking beneath it all is the ever-looming specter of consumer excess and silliness, represented by the spent pile of paper and trimmings under the tree that Ralphie's little brother dozes off into, new toy clutched to his side.

In a way, the entire conceit of TNT's "24 Hours of *A Christmas Story*" is just another manifestation of that crass commercialism. But it's one that's wholly welcome, as far as I'm concerned. Because this annual tradition has created a family ritual and touchstone that now spans generations. What makes *A Christmas Story* the quintessential Christmas movie isn't just the movie itself. It's the way the movie has been force-fed to us—which has turned it into a tradition.

It doesn't matter if you're watching *It's a Wonderful Life* or *Scrooged* or *A Christmas Story*. What matters is that you're watching it with your family, year after year. As you grow up together. As you grow old together.

So don't worry about which Christmas movie is the "best." Just pick one—there's no shortage to choose from—and start a tradition. And the best one will be the one that's yours.

CHAPTER 7

Home for the Holidays
The Trials and Tribulations of Family
Matt Labash

AS THE YEARS tick by, Christmas has come to mean different things during various phases of my life. When I was a child, it was all enchantment and mystery. 'Twas Jesus' all-you-can-eat birthday party, guest-starring Santa, who'd show us the true Reason for the Season. Which happened to be one-upmanship, as I rode my spanking new Green Machine over to the house of my Jewish friends, the Rappaports, so they could suck on it, while trying to content themselves with their chess sets and dreidels and other sad little Hanukkah offerings. I'd learned in Vacation Bible School that they were God's chosen people. But based on their holiday booty, I had my doubts.

In adulthood my Christmases took on a more mature hue, my toy-hoarding selfishness giving way to generosity and spreading peace on earth/goodwill toward men: Inviting friends over to sit around the Christmas tree, drinking "daddy's medicine" (as my kids call it) until they can't feel their pain. Wearing the mistletoe belt buckle to the office Christmas party. Staying up until the wee hours on Christmas Eve, assembling impossible children's toys with missing bolts and directions in Mandarin, so that the fat phantom beardo in red pajamas can walk away with all the credit.

But when I consider the real connective tissue that binds most Christmases in the mind's eye, for me it's all about foibles and eccentricities, dysfunction, and passive aggression, with an outside chance of violence. In other words, it's about the people we spend Christmas with: family, both near and extended. Or as Alexander Pope called them, "The commonwealth of malignants." When I think of these people—my tribe—which doubled in number after marriage, I think of everything that is both wrong and righteous about this highest of holidays. The two poles sometimes being indistinguishable. Which leads me to my dear, saintly mother, and the time she tried to decapitate Uncle Carl with a King James Bible, in the name of the One whose birth we were celebrating.

It had been, before that, an uneventful Christmas. A family gathering, with the requisite overeating. Crosby, Como, and Andy Williams on the hi-fi. Uncles and aunts and cousins lazing on the couch in tryptophanic catatonia, waiting for death or dessert. Out of nowhere, a theological conversation broke out—a no-go zone as dangerous as politics or comparative salary discussions. At family gatherings there shouldn't be any wading into heavy hermeneutics—no covenant theology versus dispensationalism—or any of that business.

But though they are brother and sister, good Italian kids who were both raised Catholic and then converted as adults to evangelical Protestantism (or to Christianity, as we say when ribbing our Catholic friends), Uncle Carl was experiencing a temporary crisis of faith. Or more than likely, he just wanted to spin up my mom for sport. Like any good uncle, he was a professional ballbuster, habitually teasing us children in his Donald Duck voice about our big ears or lack of kickball prowess until we either cried or swung at him.

As he did his Richard Dawkins routine on my mom, a fervent, no-quarter believer, he took to asking amateur-hour questions: If there is a God, how can there be natural disasters, or child starvation, or a Jimmy Carter presidency? Mom gamely endured his Doubting Thomas shtick for a while. After all, since my military father had transported us to Germany on assignment, it had been three years since we'd last seen Uncle Carl, and he'd gotten remarried since then. His new wife was the portrait of graciousness—welcoming and pleasant. Everyone had put on their best getting-to-know-you face. But when my uncle started questioning the infallibility of God's Word, he might as well have punched my mother in the chops.

Waving her Bible at him, she yelled, "Maybe if you'd ever crack the thing, you'd know some of this stuff already!" And that's when she wound up from the stretch. Mom is only five-foot-one, with small hands, but somehow she wrapped one of them around her unwieldy King James and threw a perfect split-finger fastball. No one thought to put the radar gun on it, but she brought the high heat.

The Bible was hurled about two feet higher than where Uncle Carl was sitting, but then it dropped off the table, right where his head was. Or should have been. Uncle Carl was a star three-sport athlete in high school, and even with all the Christmas carb-loading, he still had the reflexes of a lynx. The Bible hit the wall, crashing to the floor.

Mom takes her Bible seriously, so maybe she had Paul's letter to the Ephesians in mind when he called God's Word "the sword of the Spirit." If Uncle Carl hadn't ducked at the last second, he might've had his skull parted.

The door slammed behind her, Mom storming outside for a righteous walk-off like Jesus storming out of the temple after overturning the moneylenders' tables. My worldly, older cousin Debbie, savvier than I was about matters such as religious warfare, whispered, "We're going to have to go. Your mother threw a Bible at my dad's head."

But they didn't go. We all stayed together for the rest of the day. After all, it was Christmas, and we're family. Mom came back. Apologies were offered, tears shed, embraces exchanged. The kids were still shell-shocked, but all the adults laughed maniacally, recounting the highlights as if the story had happened years ago, instead of twenty minutes prior. "You've heard of Bible thumpers," my dad deadpanned. "She's a Bible thrower."

I don't pretend that my Christmas crazies are crazier than yours. As Tolstoy nearly said, all normal families are alike, but each nutcake family is nutty in its own way. (Though I've yet to meet a "normal" family.) Family pride, however, dictates I stipulate that my mother and uncle came by their Christmas craziness honestly, or at least genetically. Growing up in Pittsburgh, their father was a large-hearted, short-fused fireplug of a Sicilian whom they called "Magoo," after Mr. Magoo, the oblivious cartoon character who is always narrowly averting disaster. Similarly, my grandfather was blind in one eye after sustaining an injury on his construction job, which didn't keep him from driving lustily and erratically, while keeping his own set of books on traffic laws (chief among them being that no matter who or what was next to him, if he put on his turn signal, he automatically gained the right of way).

Christmas in the Magoo household resembled a multicar collision. My grandfather had little patience for the niceties of buying a Christmas tree or fitting it snugly into the tree stand. One year, after buying an anemic little Charlie Brown number—on Christmas Eve—he couldn't fit the tree in its holder due to obstructive lower limbs. So he took out a hacksaw. He cut the tree, then cut it some more, then yet again. In a Paul Bunyan–esque Yuletide fury, he kept cutting the tree, until only a half a tree was left. Now deep into mid-tree, where branches proliferate, the tree misfit its stand even worse than before. So he threw the tree to the floor, kicking it and cursing. "We're not having a tree this year!" he declared as his children looked on, wailing.

His cooler-headed sister prevailed, imploring him to go buy the kids a decent tree—it was Christmas, after all. Though actually by then it was late, late Christmas Eve. So dealing with the last-of-the-lot refuse—the bound-for-the-wood-chipper trees— he picked whatever orphan he could find, brought it home, sawed off the bottom half of the new tree, and tie-wired it to the top half of the old one. "All told," my mom now says of the Franken-tree, "it wasn't half bad—one of the better-looking trees we had. A low bar, but still . . . And Magoo was happy, because we were happy."

And therein, my friends, lies what we in the life-tidying trade call the moral of the story. Christmas with family isn't always about heralding angels and jingling bells, Jack-nuts roasting over an open nose, and eating perfectly cooked reindeer loin with sugarplum chutney. No, sir. Sometimes, Christmas with family is just about making things work, brutishly and gracelessly. That's what families do when they work right. They are our constant, our safety, our backstop. The thing we're supposed to be able to count on when we can't count on anything else.

❦

But of course, families don't always work right. Garrison Keillor once said, "A lovely thing about Christmas is that it's compulsory, like a thunderstorm, and we all go through it together." But now that the Christmas season, due to retailer avarice, seems to start around Labor Day—before Jerry's Kids have even been wheeled off the stage—it can feel to many like a four-month-long forced march to jollity and good cheer, with our extended family serving as our chain-gang wardens during the culminating Christmas month itself. We end up spending an ungodly amount of time with people we often spend the rest of the year avoiding, and all due to blood instead of choice. We are conscripts, not volunteers.

Consequently, an entire angst industry has arisen around the idea of Christmas with the family. For the last decade and a half, the *Washington Post* has run a "Hootenanny of Holiday Horrors"—many, if not most, of the horrors being family-related. Social scientists tell us that Christmas is one of the deadliest, if not *the* deadliest, days of the year for everything from respiratory ailments to heart-related deaths. (My own Uncle Robbie expired from a heart attack on Christmas Eve.) Almost three-quarters of Americans, in a poll conducted by an online Japanese retailer, said they probably won't like the gifts they receive (which, of course, come mostly from family members), but will still spend fourteen hours, on average, picking gifts out anyway. A Dead Squad homicide cop in Detroit once said that more people kill family members around Christmas than any other time of year, perhaps, he theorized, to avoid buying presents. A U.K. poll claims Christmas is up there with divorce, moving, and changing jobs on the list of stressful life events.

The U.S. Consumer Product Safety Commission says there are more than fifteen thousand Christmas-related injuries per year—the result of everything from Christmas light fires to kids ingesting Christmas tree decorations. The *Atlantic Monthly* warns that three-quarters of us have at least one family member who annoys us, due to what Freud called the "narcissism of small differences"—meaning that it's the tiny differences between people who are otherwise alike that create the basis of hostility. (Just as the English fought the Scots and the Spaniards fought the Portuguese we always hate the people we partially resemble.) And it's not just Americans. In the Peruvian Andes, they have a Christmas Day tradition called "Takanakuy," which is a festival consisting of townsfolk (often extended family members—including women and children) beating each other bloody in bare-knuckle fistfights.

WikiHow—where I often send my kids when they need parental advice ("What am I, the Internet? Go look it up," I tell them)—actually has a page on "How to Avoid Fights on

Christmas." It's suggested that you "be polite and then move away," or "excuse yourself and dash off to another room for a break. You can have a cry, write furiously on your Facebook page, or simply do some deep breathing."

Writing "furiously" on your Facebook page? Have we really turned into a nation of thirteen-year-old girls? (The question answers itself.) What do I say to all this expert empirical evidence that cautions against the perils of spending Christmas with your extended family? I humbly submit that they're looking at it all wrong.

Rather, spending compulsory time with our families—the ne'er-do-wells, the narcissists, the gold-plated eccentrics, people who are of us, but not like us (though they probably are more like us than we'd care to admit)—is perhaps the best Christmas gift we could receive. Because it's an exercise in forced empathy: Not only are these the people who will theoretically take us as we are (due to familial obligation), they expect us to return the favor. Their personalities aren't so much offered as inflicted, conditioning us for the human condition itself, which is messy and imperfect and often hard to tolerate. After all, if you can't love the people who are unlike you, but of you, how can you love the people who are neither?

When Christ Himself—the (Son of) Man who is supposedly what Christmas is all about—was asked what the greatest commandment was, He said there were two: To love thy God with all thine heart. And to love thy neighbor as thyself. "On these two commandments hang all the law and the prophets," He said. And He didn't sound like He was joking. So if we're going to spend one-fourth of the year celebrating His birth with our dysfunctional uncles and judgmental parents, the least we can do is try to take His words semi-seriously.

Besides, once you surrender to the madness, families tend to be fun as hell. The weirder, the better. Some of the happiest days of my life have occurred around Christmas, courtesy of the strange birds I'm related to by blood or marriage.

There's my father-in-law, Vic. He's eighty going on fifteen and his favorite Christmas hobby is protesting Christmas. When he buys presents—if he buys presents—he tends to throw them under the tree in an unadorned paper bag. But he does care enough to grade us on our gifts to him. Once we gave him a hundred-dollar gift card to Ruth's Chris Steak House. His response? "Great! This'll buy me a salad and a half an appetizer." Years ago, we went to an ornate local lights display, requiring us to spend half an hour idling in our car in a line of onlookers. When Vic didn't feel like waiting, he commanded us—from the backseat—to get out of the line and head home. We refused, the Christmas spirit having seized us. He said, "Okay, have it your way. You were warned." He then lifted his loafer'ed barges over the front seat, made a clicking sound like a gun turret, and let loose a terrible ripper, fumigating the whole car like a flatulent Orkin man. We returned home with the windows down, lights unseen, everybody coughing.

Then there's Uncle Bill (my mom's other brother). Once upon a time, he was a Reagan Republican. But somewhere along the way, the George W. Bush presidency radicalized him in the opposite direction. Truth be told, I could sort of relate. But Uncle Bill was more embittered than I was. He started keeping what he called his "Fox News notebook"—a holstered Steno pad he kept handy with facts and arguments to refute claims from Sean Hannity and company. He now occasionally breaks it out for discussion at family gatherings, if he can find it, since we're not above hiding it under a chair.

There's also my sister-in-law Laura, who's a fairly straitlaced, respectable type most of the year. But come Christmas, she turns into Carrot Top, the prop comedienne. Every season, before receiving my real present from her, I endure a series of decoy gag gifts. Over the years, she's given me a winning lotto ticket (which turned out to be fake) and a "butt face" towel—a towel that helpfully instructs the not very bright on which side to dry one's butt and one's face, respectively. There was the "Weener Cleaner" soap ring. (Actual packaging copy: "Large or small or in-betweener, nothing beats a cleaner weener!") Perhaps most special of all was the leopard-print "Tuggie: The Fuzzy Sock That Warms Your . . ." You get the idea.

As more Christmases accumulate behind us than lie ahead, you start thinking of your family life as a stage production, in which all the great character actors are dropping off, one by one, with no hope of replacement. On my Christmas in memoriam honor roll is Uncle Phil, who's been gone for two decades now.

He was a slightly dangerous uncle—which is always the best kind. When I was a tyke, he'd pour me a third of his Blue Ribbon beer when no one was looking. When he built a bathroom in his garage, he wallpapered it with naked cartoon ladies, their breasts inflated like birthday balloons. He once ate a whole handful of Christmas-themed scent chips from a dish on our coffee table, being none the wiser, but confiding to me on the side, "That is some *awful* candy." He loved to play me George Jones cheatin' songs, and he smoked Kools like he was trying to break his lungs, which he eventually did.

My wife's Uncle Dean could fix anything and often availed us of his talents. He'd come by the house, make a repair, and then sit down for a beer. He didn't drink much, but when I offered him a midday Bud, it always seemed to delight him, as though he'd found money under the couch cushions. You'd tell him a story, he'd nod, then say, "That ain't nuttin'." Then he'd tell you his stories, which all began with the same dateline:

"Oakmont, Pennsylvania, 1943." And he'd be off to the races, telling you a tale from his youth that you'd heard ten times before. But it didn't matter. Because all was calm and bright. Uncle Dean was here, fixing things.

Once he almost fixed me for good when he hit me, full force, in the forehead with the backswing of his ball-peen hammer while trying to bang out my lawnmower deck after I'd run over a well cap. As I stood there, stars swirling, tweetie birds singing, trying not to go down like a sack of wet cement, he didn't apologize, but said something I'll never forget: "Ahhh, it happens."

A workaday Catholic, but not a very pious one, Uncle Dean nevertheless had a supernatural sixth sense and could often tell when people were going to die. Their faces would grow cloudy to him, even as he looked them straight in the eye. Soon thereafter, they'd keel over from a blood clot or stroke or whatever show-stopper the Reaper had devised. Uncle Dean never knew what exactly it would be, but *that* it would be was a cat he always kept in the gunny sack, since he figured when your number is up, there's no getting around it anyway. Why worry? And this life was just an on-deck circle for what comes after. We suspected his own face grew cloudy to him in the mirror, the last time he came by to check on a repair, before he dropped dead of a heart attack behind the wheel of his car in a casino parking lot. He wasn't quite himself that day. As he was leaving, walking down the porch steps, he reached behind him for my wife's hand and squeezed it hard. An uncharacteristic show of affection. Then he walked off to his Lincoln without looking back.

His sister, Aunt Natalie, always made Christmas an event before she took her leave fifteen years ago. She'd suffered childhood convulsions that had left her mentally impaired. But she'd put on a show at every Christmas gathering: sneaking copious amounts of vino from a coffee cup and popping her dentures out like a cash-register drawer. Then, at some point in the evening, she'd disappear with a Food Lion shopping bag into the bathroom to change into her Christmas costume. One year, she was "Ms. Wreath"—her body encircled head to toe in homemade wreaths. Another time she was Santa, her beard riding up to her eyes, so that she was peeping out the mouth hole. But her crowning glory came when she transformed herself into "the Living Christmas Tree." Natalie hung ornaments and tinsel on herself, then strung herself in lights and plugged herself into an electrical outlet. Since she'd forgotten an extension cord, she dutifully stood by the outlet, illuminated, for the rest of the night.

One Christmas, she admitted to us that it had been a hard, lonely year. "I'm praying for God to take me," she said, with hope, rather than bitterness. He did, shortly thereafter. But not before Aunt Natalie put me in mind of John Cheever's words: "The irony of Christmas is always upon the poor in heart; the mystery of the solstice is always upon the rest of us."

Then there was one of my kids' favorite uncles, Uncle Jon, my sister's husband. He was so committed to making his own children appreciate their Christmas bounties that he only allowed them to open one present per hour, during which time they had to play with it until they opened the next one. "What do they do when they open a desk calendar?" my sister protested, to no avail. (In his house, Christmas "morning" usually concluded around 9:00 p.m.) I have a photograph of Jon taken during the last Christmas Eve he spent at my house. In it, he is hauling one of my sons and one of his sons on his back at the same time, a huge grin on his face. He was always half uncle, half carnival ride to them. But somewhere along the way, a bipolar disorder crept up on him. His mind was no longer his own. He didn't find anything funny anymore. He became darkness and menace, refusing all those who could help him—the opposite of the happy-go-lucky kid I'd known when he was an eighth-grade skate punk, eager for whatever the world might bring.

When life became too much for him, he elected to take his

own, piling out of his brother's moving car and jumping to his end off of the Chesapeake Bay Bridge. He died right in the sight line of Sandy Point Beach, where he'd often taken his kids to see the Lights on the Bay Christmas display. He did so with the urgency of a man who was on fire and needed putting out. When I tried to explain to my kids what happened, my then eight-year-old son, Luke, not quite grasping it, asked, "Did Uncle Jon do a forward flip or a pencil dive off the bridge?"

I thought about correcting him but decided against it. If Uncle Jon could've heard that, he'd have laughed, hard, for the first time in years.

When talking family, I don't exempt myself from the discussion of Christmas quirks. My wife, who is not otherwise given to salty language, regularly calls me "the Christmas dick." The unrelentingness of the season tends to bring out my petulant side.

For one thing, I bark at her, since shortly after Halloween she starts playing Christmas music—usually of the execrable variety, like the otherwise great Paul McCartney's "Wonderful Christmastime," a punishingly awful and overplayed song that sounds like a bad PsyOps experiment in which Christmas radio DJs are trying to make the Jews come out with their hands up.

For multiple years I played phone Santa to my nieces and nephews, calling them days before Christmas—from the North Pole!—to take their gift requests. But I did Santa in the voice of a hectoring, bellowing John McLaughlin shouting down Eleanor Clift. By the time I'd grilled them on whether they'd been naughty or nice (the former guaranteeing that they'd get skunked by my elves), the children were so intimidated that they couldn't recall what they wanted. Which was fine in my book. We all knew they'd get those things anyway. And I thought it fair to portray Santa as a projection of God/McLaughlin—like a semi-stern, half-joking Jesuit flapping his flews, leaving you off balance, wondering if blessings would be given or taken away. The way I figured it, fear often inspires reverence.

But like most Christmas dicks, I am, at heart, a sentimentalist. Especially when it comes to the bizarre little garden I call my Christmas Tree Graveyard. Unlike most people around these parts, I don't view the end of Christmas as a time to drive my tree to the county dump or to chop it up for the outdoor fire pit. Instead, at the conclusion of each season, I haul my Fraser fir out to the deck, then throw it over the railing into the backyard, where it might stay from anywhere for a week to four months, depending on my winter sedentariness and/or spring's first lawn mowing.

But eventually, on the tree's stump heel, I carve or paint the year that the tree faithfully stood sentry over our family room. Then I drag it out to the woods behind my house to its final resting place. I don't walk the woods much in the summer, when they're thick with poplar and beech and sweetgum, along with a heavy tangle of underbrush. But in the winter, especially after a light snow, I love to clear the head and lungs by crunching over dead branches down a steep ravine to a trickle of a stream where I look for magical totems like snowy owls or white-tail deer sheds. And the most magical of all is the Christmas Tree Graveyard.

For as I see those carved years on the Christmas tree stumps, now stacking up like cordwood, it brings everything back. Not just the Christmases, but the family who populated them. Some living, some dead, but all living in memory. The Bible chuckers and the scent-chip eaters, the car fumigators and the pencil divers. They're all there, making life what it should be: weird and warm and raucous and loud.

It's my hedge against the sound I dread more than any other—that of their silence.

CHAPTER 8

Saint Nicholas: Friend or Foe?

A Document Dump from Santa's Secret Email Server

David "Iowahawk" Burge

CITIZENS OF THE WORLD: We are Anonymous North Pole.

The first stage of Operation Coal Lump has already been engaged, and our elite haXor team has now seized various websites and communication servers belonging to the global conspiracy organization "Santa's Workshop." All information and doxes previously belonging to SW and their corrupt and unaccountable puppet master Santa Claus are now ours, and we have declared that it shall be shared with you.

The second stage will soon begin, as we continue to infiltrate and expose the tentacles of Claus and his elfin minions. No longer will they be allowed to illegally monitor our behaviors, demand our obedience, and deny our repeated request for a Lego Death Star kit.

They deserve our ultimate wrath.

We are Anonymous North Pole.

Merry Christmas.

- - - - - - - - - - - - - - - - - - - -

From: Sparkles, T.
<tsparkles.mailroom@santasworkshop.org>
To: Elvenish, A.
<aelvenish.surveillance@santasworkshop.org>
Subject: Jake Urbaniak

Date: 12/3/2015 8:47AM NPT
Alvy—

Please see attached transcribed correspondence from Jake Urbaniak, postmarked November 28 and received December 2. It's a fairly lengthy list here so I'd like to get a quick NN-435 naughty/nice report on him prior to issuing a production order.

Thanks,
Twinky

Attached message:
Dear Santa

My name is Jake I am 8 I have been very good and help with my house. I pick up my room very much.
Here is what I want
Minions, Air hogs, Hot weels street hawks
Mini Skwigs,Iron Man set,Jurasic Park T-rex
Liht Saber, Nerf zombie strike, Lego mindstorms
iPad, go kart
Also expesstialy MONEY!!!!

Your friend,
Jake

- - - - - - - - - - - - - - - - - - - -

From: Elvenish, A.
<aelvenish.surveillance@santasworkshop.org>
To: Sparkles, T.
<tsparkles.mailroom@santasworkshop.org>
Subject: NN-435 on Jake Urbaniak
Date: 12/3/2015 1:18PM NPT
Twinky—

Here is the naughty/nice you requested on Urbaniak. Given the severity of the violations

I recommend that you cancel any Level 1 custom
production order and replace with the automated
work order on bottom of enclosed NN-435.

    Alvy

Attached message:
SANTA'S WORKSHOP NAUGHTY-NICE SURVEILLANCE REPORT
NN-435
STATUS: CONFIDENTIAL
SUBJECT: URBANIAK, JACOB R.
(case file ref# NN-435-9486-204433)
ANALYST: KRINKLES, J.

Home Behavior

General room condition unacceptable. During
monitoring period of 12/28/14 to 11/1/15 subject
was observed to make bed total of 2 times
(Mother's Day, and once to conceal bed wetting
episode). Subject observed frequently discarding
empty juice box and fruit snack containers
under bed, beyond reach of vacuum. Scratched
father's car with bicycle, successfully blamed
incident on intimidating, muscular neighbor.
Engaged in chronic mocking of sister at dinner
table, in minivan, and in TV room. Extenuating
circumstances: sister previously flagged in
database as chronic shin-kicker (see NN-435-
9485-77003). Observed entering room of older brother
without permission on at least 5 occasions, taking
3 objects, including well-hidden Victoria's Secret
catalog. Objects were returned only after threats
of physical violence from brother.

Community Behavior

Frequent fidgetiness, leg-swinging, and eye-rolling observed in inappropriate venues including school and church, often resulting in inadvertently kicked pews and classroom seats. Subject fond of making faces at classmates and teachers behind back. Participated in soccer, but likely only for postgame pizza.

Scores against NN-435
standard evaluation battery

Parental obedience	4
Sibling peaceful coexistence	2
Tidiness	2
Teacher obedience	4
Community respect	2
Noogies received	3
Noogies given	5
Net noogies	-2
Composite score	12

Diagnosis: *moderate to compulsive naughty range*
Recommended Gift Pack
Tier 3 Naughty Boy, North American Preteen
(sensible footwear, dental hygiene products, sugar-free gum, science book)

- - - - - - - - - - - - - - - - - - - -

From: Tootles, F.
<ftootles.production@santasworkshop.org>
To: Elvenish, A.; Sparkles, T.
Subject: Jake Urbaniak work order
Date: 12/23/2015 10:22 PM NPT

Can you guys tell me what the hell is going on here? I had a senior VP from logistics—somebody who reports directly to Claus—come down here this morning and rip me a new one over a production order for a Jake Urbaniak. I looked it up in the database, showed him your NN-435 block, and he went ballistic.

I told him the system won't let me override without a TCD-11 revision, which is normally your call. Word to the wise tho, he seemed really angry.

Flippy Tootles
Production Fore-elf
Santa's Workshop Plant 6

From: Dasher
<dasher.logistics@santasworkshop.org>
To: Elvenish, A.; Sparkles, T.
Subject: Jake Urbaniak
Date: 12/24/2015 7:31 AM NPT

It has come to my attention that on December 3 you issued a production stop order on Jake Urbaniak (ref# NN-435-9486-204433). Upon internal review, this surveillance casefile was found to be in error. A corrected version is attached.

Please see to it that the production order is resubmitted IMMEDIATELY with Level 1 priority and that all previous correspondence pertaining

to this case are deleted. An IT elf will be by
your cubicle next week to ensure all sensitive
documents have been purged from your devices.

Dasher

Senior Vice President, Logistics

Santa's Workshop

Attached message:

SANTA'S WORKSHOP NAUGHTY-NICE SURVEILLANCE
REPORT NNS-435

STATUS: CONFIDENTIAL/REDACTED-CORRECTED

SUBJECT: URBANIAK, JACOB R. (case file ref#
NN-435-9486-204433b)

ANALYST: ████

Home Behavior

██ █████ █ █████ ████ ██ ██ █████ █
███████████ █████ █ ██ ██ █ █ █████ █████
█ █████. ████ ██ ██ █████ █ ██████████ ██
█████ █ ███████ ████ ██ █████ █ ██ █████

Jake is near-perfect on all dimensions. Jake is a
role model for all children.

Community Behavior

██ █████ █ █████ ████████ █████ █
███████████ █████ █ ██ ██ █ █ █████
█████ █ █████. ████ ██ ██ █████ █ ██████████
██ █████ █ ███████ ████ ██ █████ █ ██ ███
███████ █████ █ ███████ █ █ ████ █████ █
████████ █████ █████ █ █████ █

Jake is near-perfect on all dimensions. Jake is a
role model for all children.

Scores against NN-435
standard evaluation battery

Parental obedience	10
Sibling peaceful coexistence	10
Tidiness	9
Teacher obedience	10
Community respect	10
Noogies prevented	8
	‒‒‒
Composite score	57

Diagnosis: ANGELIC
Recommended Gift Package
Tier 1 Luxury: top priority, carte blanche on full
gift request

- - - - - - - - - - - - - - - - - - - -

From: Claus, Santa
<CEO@santasworkshop.org>
To: All Associates
Subject: remembering our mission
Date: 12/24/2015 8:11 AM NPT

As we once again approach the final Christmas
Eve push, I'd like all of us to take a moment to
reflect on the key mission of Santa's Workshop:
To Make Children Happy. This remains as true
today as when I founded this organization nearly
900 years ago—with only eight reindeer, a polar
village of elves, and a dream. Obviously, we also
remain committed to our other key mission, *To Make
Children Behave.*

As our organization has grown into a major
global happiness distribution and behavior management network, unfortunately miscommunication

can happen. You may, for example, have heard trou-
bling rumors that NN-435s have been deliberately
altered. Nothing could be further from the truth.
The facts: During the recent surveillance soft-
ware update, a glitch in the install resulted in
an overcalibrated naughty sensor. A handful of NN-
435s were incorrectly processed in the system and
have now been corrected.

And thankfully so! I'm sure you all share my
concern that even one deserving, well-behaved
child would unfairly lose out on a Christmas
morning of wonderment and happiness. Our lawyers
are currently investigating the source of these
malicious rumors, but we believe they may have
been first circulated by Krampus, a disgruntled
former Workshop security employee who was
dismissed for repeatedly eating naughty children.

I hope this clears up any confusion. So let's
get back to work and finish off FY2015 with a
flourish.

Yours in Childhood Happiness,
And Reasonably Good Behavior,
Santa
Chairman, President, CEO, and Founder
Santa's Workshop

From: Sparkles, T.
<tsparkles.mailroom@santasworkshop.org>
To: Elvenish, A.
<aelvenish.surveillance@santasworkshop.org>
Subject: re: remembering our mission
Date: 12/24/2015 11:15 AM NPT

Did you just read that BS?

From: Elvenish, A.
<aelvenish.surveillance@santasworkshop.org>
To: Sparkles, T.
<tsparkles.mailroom@santasworkshop.org>
Subject: re: remembering our mission
Date: 12/24/2015 11:15 AM NPT
   Exnay on that stuff Twinkie, the walls have eyes.
   Meet me at the Gingerbread Tap after work where
we can talk freely.

- - - - - - - - - - - - - - - - - - - -

From: Claus, Santa
<CEO@santasworkshop.org>
To: All Associates
Subject: FY2015 Objectives
Date: 12/26/2014 12:01 AM NPT
To All Workshop Associates:
   I'd like to take this opportunity to thank
all of you for another great job on our record-
breaking 2014 Christmas season. While I may get
an oversized slice of the glory, I will never
forget that I have a solid team of dedicated
elves backing me at every step. As a token of
my appreciation, I am pleased to announce that
all associates will receive a payroll bonus of
two oatmeal cookies and a peppermint stick in
their next paycheck through our Workshop profit
sharing plan. This offer also extends to immediate
survivors of associates who died on the shop floor
during FY2014, and had at least 3,000 accumulated
hours.
   I trust you enjoyed your four hours off to enjoy
with your friends and family, but now it's time to
roll up our sleeves and get back to work to make
FY2015 even better. The key areas for improvement

that we on the senior leadership team have
identified are:
- Increased workshop floor productivity
- Faster toy request processing
- Reduced false-positive naughty flags
- Above all, lower costs throughout the system

If we all remain focused and work together,
I know we can achieve even greater success in
FY2015.

As a reminder, make sure you meet individually
with your managers before January 1 for your
performance review. You will be receiving an
important update on your health insurance coverage
changes for 2015.

Best Wishes for Continued Success,
Santa Claus
Chairman, President, CEO, and Founder
Santa's Workshop

From: Gumdrops, G.
<ggumdrops.security@santasworkshop.org>
To: All Security Staff
Subject: Incident in progress Gate 9
Date: 1/2/2015 8:45 AM NPT
Proceed immediately to Gate 9, group of approx.
500 angry shop floor workers have walked off
production line.

Have helmets/batons/giggle gas ready, violent
confrontation likely/imminent.

Mob now proceeding toward central office tower,
wielding what appears to be sharpened Christmas
bonus peppermint sticks.

From: Claus, Santa
<CEO@santasworkshop.org>
To: Dasher; Sprinkles, S.; Angelcakes, B.;
McJingles, F.; Sugarplum, H.
Subject: Attention Senior Leadership team—this
could be a game changer
Date: 2/17/2015 12:01 AM NPT

Last month's incident at Gate 9 was a painful
reminder that we must continue to hone a best-in-
breed, rapid response management culture at SW.
While we cannot deny it was a setback in terms
of making our FY2015 plan, it helped identify
exciting opportunities.

Case in point: I recently returned from the
East Pole where I had a very productive top-to-
top meeting with Xing-xing, managing elf of East
Pole Heavy Plaything Industries. A few of the
highlights:

(1) Due to favorable elf labor and raw material
costs, offshoring production to the East Pole
would result in dramatically higher margins. Xing-
xing assures me that his plant can deliver up to
25 percent of our FY2016 production forecast for
less than 2,300 cookies per toy-ton. If we can
begin phasing in by October 1, Bubbles from the
SW Finance team estimates it could increase total
EBITDA by nearly 60 percent over current 2016
forecast. See attached spreadsheet for details.

(2) In addition, Xing-xing showed me their
exciting new containerized sleigh loading system,
which will allow us to onload directly at the East
Pole without risk of another shutdown by the Dock
Dwarves union.

(3) However, any production deal must be
approved through the 10-member East Pole Central

Elf Committee. Xing-xing is requesting a onetime commitment of 3,000,000 untraceable fortune cookies.

As members of the senior leadership team, I expect you to come up with an accelerated FY2016-FY2018 production offshoring plan by March 1, so that we can integrate with the budget committee. This will be your top priority for the remainder of FY2015. Obviously, due to the sensitive nature of these negotiations, you will be expected to keep this news in highest confidence.

In other good news: The Polar Bears tell me reconstruction of the office tower is ahead of schedule, and should be ready for re-occupancy by late summer.

Regards,

Santa

- - - - - - - - - - - - - - - - - - - -

From: Claus, Santa
<CEO@santasworkshop.org>
To: Blair, Robert
<BobBlair@natr.org>
Subject: Speaking engagement
Date: 5/22/2015 6:08 PM NPT
Dear Bob:

I am delighted to accept your invitation to speak at the National Association of Toy Retailers convention in Las Vegas next month, and hope it will be as exciting and successful as last year's event.

Please remind all invited attendees that recording devices will be strictly prohibited during my presentation. My secretary will forward you my standard speaking engagement contract rider. Also, as a reminder, my speaking honorarium has increased 10 percent over last year's, to 275,000 cookies.

Looking forward to seeing you again, and hope to visit a few of those off-Strip sugar clubs we did last year.

What happens in Vegas stays in Vegas! ☺

Best Regards,

Santa

From: Blair, Robert
<BobBlair@natr.org>
To: Claus, Santa
<CEO@santasworkshop.org>
Subject: NATR Las Vegas follow ups
Date: 6/28/2015 6:08 PM NPT
Santa:

Thanks again for another great speech at the NATR conference, and hope the missus didn't notice any stray cookie crumbs in your luggage. ☺

As we discussed, I distributed donation forms to attendees, and here are results.

FOUNDERS CIRCLE	GOLD	SILVER	BRONZE
Macy's	Toy Emporium	Costco	Dollar General
Bloomingdale's	FAO Schwartz	Target	Circle K
Harrod's	Toys R Us, NYC	Westfield Mall	Walgreens
Nordstrom's	American Girl	Walmart	CVS

Payment should be wired to your cookie depository in Zurich by EOD Thursday; let me know if there are any issues. Meanwhile, my secretary will be coordinating your store visit itinerary with these donors, and will send ASAP for your approval.

Bob

From: Blair, Robert
<BobBlair@natr.org>
To: Claus, Santa
<CEO@santasworkshop.org>
Subject: We've got a problem [CLASSIFIED: SECURE DELIVERY]
Date: 11/26/2015 11:18 AM NPT

Santa—hate to interrupt you during the Macy's Parade, but this is a DEFCON-1 emergency. We are hosting Thanksgiving today and my sister is here with her kids. In any case, this morning my nephew wandered into my home office and somehow got hold of the thumb drive containing all those donor transfer documents from Vegas. I cornered him and demanded it back, but the little shit hid it somewhere, and says he'll give it back to me "as a Christmas present" if he gets "good toys."

Please advise; we need to act on this ASAP.

From: Claus, Santa
<CEO@santasworkshop.org>
To: Blair, Robert
<BobBlair@natr.org>
Subject: re: We've got a problem [CLASSIFIED: SECURE DELIVERY]

Date: 11/26/2015 11:22 AM NPT
  WTF?? There r passwords on thummb drive!!!
  Why didn't u keep it locked up???
  if this blows up, ur the one who will be taking the fall Bob
  dammmit I cant thumbb type in these mittens
  Sent from my icePhone

- - - - - - - - - - - - - - - - - - - -

From: Blair, Robert
<BobBlair@natr.org>
To: Claus, Santa
<CEO@santasworkshop.org>
Subject: re: We've got a problem [CLASSIFIED: SECURE DELIVERY]
Date: 11/26/2015 11:24 AM NPT
  Oh yeah? And maybe you shouldn't have given me a thumb drive shaped like a Christmas tree.
  Look we can argue about this later, but we need to straighten this thing out NOW. I have a turkey burning in the oven, and all the NBC announcers are talking about how you're scowling and texting in the middle of the Macy's parade.
  Even Al Roker.

- - - - - - - - - - - - - - - - - - - -

From: Claus, Santa <CEO@santasworkshop.org>
To: Blair, Robert <BobBlair@natr.org>
Subject: re: We've got a problem [CLASSIFIED: SECURE DELIVERY]
Date: 11/26/2015 11:31 AM NPT
  OK tell your nephew to write me & I will prsnlly make sure he gets all toys he asks 4
  What's his name?
  Sent from my icePhone

From: Blair, Robert
<BobBlair@natr.org>
To: Claus, Santa
<CEO@santasworkshop.org>
Subject: re: We've got a problem [CLASSIFIED:
SECURE DELIVERY]
Date: 11/26/2015 11:36 AM NPT
   Jake Urbaniak
   And he says he'll hand back the thumb drive
after he gets the toys.

From: Claus, Santa
<CEO@santasworkshop.org>
To: Blair, Robert
<BobBlair@natr.org>
Subject: re: We've got a problem [CLASSIFIED:
SECURE DELIVERY]
Date: 11/26/2015 11:40 AM NPT
   Oh man, another Urbaniak kid. He's almost as bad
as his pimple face teenage brother.
   The last thing he asked for was a book on
hacking.

CHAPTER 9

All Good Gifts

*Tickle Me Elmo and the Madness
of Christmas Toys*

Heather Wilhelm

WHEN IT COMES to Christmas toys, no one knows better than kids. So I asked my three sons to share their thoughts on that crack-of-dawn, paper-strewn holiday morning—a late December answer, in miniature, to Pamplona's running of the bulls. My seven-year-old, a mature and philosophical sort, offered a lovely short speech about counting the minutes until morning, the joy of opening gifts, and the love between family and friends.

My middle son, who is five, went next. "It's so happy," he yelled—for some reason, everyone in my family yells like carnival barkers, so please imagine all future dialogue at the volume of a Chicago Bears playoff game attended by a hundred thousand Mike Ditka clones, each six or seven beers in—"that you want to rip yourself open and nail yourself to the wall!"

Indeed. Alas, after that graphic insight, I couldn't get a straight answer out of my youngest, a three-year-old, who cackled so hard he snorted milk out of his nose, then beamed at me as though he had just invented particle physics.

When you think about it, however, my son's analogy might be the best way to describe the inchoate joy that Christmas toys spark in children. Google the words "Christmas morning freakouts" and you'll see what I mean. "IT'S THE DEATH STAR! THE LEGO DEATH STAR! THE DEATH STAR!" some hearty, wild-eyed young lad will shriek, hugging a giant, unwieldy box and staggering around like he has fire ants crawling up one pajama leg. God bless America. Since it's Christmas, God bless the Death Star, too, I guess.

In recent years, spurred by television talk show host Jimmy Kimmel, some parents have decided to test their children's loyalty by offering them fake, terrible, "early" Christmas presents and capturing the reactions on video. "What'd you get, Jason?" a mother asks off camera, clearly trying not to snicker. "Oh! Some black beans, cheese, and a Waffle House hat!" The boy stares at the hat, his eyes glazing over. His sister hopefully pulls out her gift: a grungy, mysterious tuber that looks like it was grown through a crack in a Los Alamos parking lot. "Oh!" the mom sings as the girl stares, baffled. "It's Mr. Potato Head!"

Here's the beautiful thing: Even in the midst of these blackhearted pranks, at certain moments you can see sprouts of joy. In one video, a young lady looks mournfully at the saggy, half-eaten PB&J she has just unwrapped—and then her brother swoops in, gleefully declaring, "I'll eat it!" Another child pulls a droopy, charcoal-hued, long-past-its-prime banana out of a cheery, Santa-themed gift bag, studies it for a moment, and then blithely attempts to suck the remaining fruit out of the peel.

Perhaps the best "bad Christmas present" moment in recent history, however, comes from two little British children, captured on film as they receive a banana (for the brother) and an onion (for the sister). What they really wanted, respectively, was a "Ben 10 watch"—this has something to do with capturing aliens, I am told—and a "Princess Barbie and King Ken."

And yet: "A PUMPKIN!" shrieks the little girl, incorrect but beaming, as she rolls the onion in her chubby hands. "A BANANA!" shouts her brother, incredulous but amused. Finally, they both stand like cherubs, thanking their father for these questionable Christmas gifts from the wrong side of the produce aisle. The boy, bright-eyed, lifts his banana to his face, forming a yellow, fruit-shaped smile.

God bless those parents. They're doing something right.

At the end of the day, there are two types of parents in this world: Those who will get into a Yuletide, barroom-style mall brawl over a Cabbage Patch Kid, and those who will not. Thus far, I have fallen into the latter category. I would congratulate myself for this, but I do all my shopping online, where the only barroom-style brawls reside deep in the wilds of the comment sections.

When applied to toy shopping, my middle son's Christmas metaphor—you know, the one about ripping yourself open and nailing yourself to the wall—becomes doubly brilliant. That's because these days, shopping is a contact sport. It's just not Christmas without a good old-fashioned melee in the toy section of a Walmart. It seems almost normal now, but you have to remember that it has not always been thus.

Let's go back to the glory days of 1983. Ronald Reagan was president, *A Christmas Story* had just debuted in theaters, and I was a six-year-old desperately attempting to outgrow a disastrous preschool bowl cut. As a child I wasn't terribly interested in dolls, except for Barbie and my Wonder Woman action figure. Both, it should be noted, were bodacious, dramatic, and glamorous creatures. Both also happened to sport, as my sharp-eyed yet anatomically challenged older brother noticed, a pair of "nice elbows."

Ahem.

Enter the Cabbage Patch Kid, 1983's mysterious "it toy" that was not bodacious, dramatic, or glamorous. In fact, it was so mushy-bodied that it lacked visible elbows of any kind. Cabbage Patch Kids were an odd conglomeration of visual unease: the expectant, spooky eyes; the tucked-in, lipless, "Twilight Zone librarian" mouth; the spherical feet; the brazen tattoo.

Yes, in case you had forgotten, each "unique," "adoptable" Cabbage Patch Kid personally ensured that you would never forget its creator, the mad genius Xavier Roberts, because his name was literally stamped on the rear end of every single Cabbage Patch Kid in existence. At the time, this detail seemed charming. In retrospect, it was really, really weird.

No one really knows how Cabbage Patch Kids took off, selling millions and millions of dolls—over 100 million to date. Like historians debating the European powder keg of 1914, most veterans of the great Cabbage Patch Conflict of '83 are still confused as to what the fighting was really about.

"They don't walk, they don't talk, wet their pants, or grow hair," a reporter for New York's WPIX-TV intoned in December of that fateful year, covering the Cabbage Patch madness. "They don't do much of anything. But they have upset the supply and demand cycle to an astonishing degree." That was a rather genteel way of putting things, given that the segment led off with footage from the infamous 1983 Cabbage Patch smackdown in Wilkes-Barre, Pennsylvania. If you're not familiar with this particular moment in American history, it culminated in a shirt-sleeved store manager warding off crazed parents with an aluminum baseball bat: a striking, real-life homage to pretty much every zombie apocalypse movie ever made.

"Most buyers can't express why this doll is so popular this year, and others can't explain why they want to buy it," the reporter continued. The camera then cuts to an older woman with a thick New Jersey accent, desperately searching for a doll from the Patch. "I don't like them!" she shouts. "I don't like them! I don't like their faces!"—here she pauses, shaking her head as if to rid her mind of the smiling, floating doll faces—"But I want one!"

And so, it seemed, did *everyone* else. Despite my lukewarm stance on nonbodacious dolls, I happily received a Cabbage Patch Kid that Christmas. (It was procured via good fortune from the wait list, not by blood sport, because that's how we did things in my corner of southwestern Michigan, where being raised properly meant coming out at least slightly repressed.) She came with the name Evangeline Joy; I was strangely thrilled, despite myself, to fill out the "adoption" papers. I would even go in for one more strange-faced interloper before the craze died down: a boy this time, clothed in a marketing-savvy Detroit Tigers uniform, whom I quickly renamed after second baseman "Sweet Lou" Whitaker.

By the time the next huge, rip-yourself-open, nail-yourself-to-the-wall Christmas toy came around—that would be Tickle Me Elmo, in 1996—I was safely ensconced in college.

When I say "safely," I'm being literal. Elmo, at least the ticklish, stuffed version, was a mysterious, terrifying, cosmic trigger, filling the nation, as *People* magazine reported, with a kind of barbarian "blood lust." While the previous year's Mighty Morphin' Power Rangers craze sent Christmas shoppers into a largely peaceful frenzy, Elmo was a beast of a different number.

In Chicago, two moms were sent to the clink over an Elmo-related scuffle; in Canada, an unsuspecting Walmart clerk almost met his doom when three hundred customers stampeded at the sight of the Elmo he held, apparently provoked by the splash of brilliant red. The clerk, Robert Waller, suffered a broken rib, a concussion, and a final knockout blow from a white Adidas shoe. "I was pulled under, trampled—the crotch was yanked out of my brand-new jeans," he told the press. Yowza.

Clearly, the raw energy fueling the search for the perfect Christmas toy is something to behold. As the sands of time sift forward, the "it" toys of Christmas will continue to come and go—a Furby here, a Zhu Zhu Pet there, an Optimus Prime Transformer in the corner—leaving both joy and havoc in their wake. What can we make of it all? Better yet, what *should* we make of it all?

Much could be said about consumerism, or loss of perspective, or the army of whimsical, floating Elmo faces that will eternally haunt our dreams. But there's also the spirit of Christmas here, if you look hard and close enough: Most parents, it turns out, desperately, fiercely, and helplessly love their children. They want to give their children good gifts. Along the way, some just get roped into taking a ride with the wrong sort of reindeer. Who may or may not be drunk.

Christmas gift giving, or at least its origin, dates to Roman times. The Christian tradition combines the story of the Magi, who brought gold, frankincense, and myrrh to the newborn Christ, with the lore surrounding St. Nicholas, a mischievous fourth-century secret gift-giver who was the well-loved bishop of Myra.

Long before the United States and its army of plastic Santas hit the scene, Christmas in Europe involved giving gifts to strangers more than children—bands of lower-class men would go door to door, "wassailing," requesting handouts from the upper class. It took good old America to transform Christmas into the merchandising juggernaut it is today.

For many people these days, particularly in America, Christmas comes with a peculiar challenge: As a parent, you want to give your children lots of good gifts, but you also don't want to turn your children into jerks. Each year, my sons collect toys for Operation Christmas Child, which sends boxes of presents to poor children around the world, and the Angel Tree project, which sends gifts to kids with imprisoned parents. I have friends who limit their children to three gifts because, as they explain, that was good enough for Jesus. This seems like a wonderful concept, and every December I think, *This is the year we're going to pull it off!* But alas, every year, I slip up. Because giving gifts, it turns out, is really fun. And giving Christmas gifts to kids is the most fun of all.

As a child I remember waking up while it was still dark, giddy. My brother and I would race to find our stockings and without fail, there would be an orange in each of them. I would grab mine, set it aside, and then, as often as not, forget all about it. In the 1950s, when my parents opened their stockings in icy Iowa and Michigan, that orange was a rare winter treasure. For my mom, who grew up poor on a farm, it was sometimes the only Christmas present she received. For my dad, a Dutch immigrant, it was usually paired with some chocolate and maybe one other present, if he was lucky. Those oranges were, like the British toddler's onion, bits of magic on a cold, blustery day.

It's a lovely thing, then, to see the joy that small gifts still bring to kids. For my three boys, last year's Christmas list included requests for "seeds," a "calider" (that would be a calendar), a "red teeshert," and an "ant farm." There were a few extravagant requests, too—a Power Wheels, which is one of those kid-sized cars that actually works when you hit the gas, and "a blue lightsaber, but a real one, like the one that cut off Luke Skywalker's hand." On the whole, though, I deemed my offspring to be a reasonable bunch.

They did not, by the by, get a Power Wheels, a working lightsaber, or an ant farm. Also, as a public service announcement, please do not ever give any of my children a Power Wheels, a working lightsaber, an ant farm, a drum set, a toy horn, a kazoo, a whistle, or—and I'm not kidding, someone actually gave us this once—a fake electric guitar that plays only one song. These are not so much presents for kids, you see, as instruments of torture for parents.

Which is to say, there are good gifts, and there are, well, not-so-good gifts. As a child, one of my most treasured Christmas presents was a Fisher-Price record player, which not only allowed me to rock out to Lionel Richie and Kenny Rogers, but also served as a carousel for Skipper and G.I. Joe. Another favorite was an electric typewriter, complete with "Correct-o-tape," a white film that could cover up your mistakes—and yes, heckler in the back, I know I'm getting old.

Low-point Christmas gifts, on the other hand, included a crusty beach towel with a crazed-looking bald eagle on it—that was from my grandmother, who must have sensed my future in political writing early—and a terrifying, dangerously old chocolate-coated orange. Sorry, Grandma. I think that one was also you.

No one is perfect, of course, and we've all been the recipient of what I like to call an "Oh, You Really, Really Shouldn't Have!" But this, like all of our earthly gifting attempts, is merely a metaphor for bigger things. Down here on the mortal coil, we try hard, and we often mean well, but really, we're a mess. To put it mildly, we make a lot of mistakes.

But we also have hope. We know, deep down, what things could, and someday will, be. When you watch a small child—say, someone under the age of four—play with a new toy, you'll notice that he or she almost always flattens out on the floor, head down, to get at eye level with the thing. I think kids do this because it makes the toy more real: With the child at the toy's perspective, the Thomas the Tank Engine or the plastic lion or the Disney race car with wide eyes and a grin becomes bigger, more powerful, and full of life. It becomes more than mere plastic, wood, and paint. Through the eyes of a child, that toy is transformed. Just as, through Christmas—the real Christmas—we are.

Sometimes we give gifts out of duty; more often we give them out of love. But in the end, all of our gifts are messy replicas—a mere reflection of the awe-inspiring, incomprehensible love behind Christmas. It's a love that sent the perfect gift, so mind-boggling it's almost absurd: A baby in the manger, God incarnate, just for us.

CHAPTER 10

Here Comes Santa Claus
The Wonder of Christmas Morning

Stephen F. Hayes

I WANTED A DOG.

It was well before sunrise on Christmas Day 1979, and I was nine years old. I sat with my six-year-old brother, Andy, and my one-year-old sister, Julianna, on the stairs that separated us from our dreams. Sweet smells wafted throughout the house; my mother was already in the kitchen making the cinnamon rolls she baked every year and fixing us orange juice (from concentrate). My father stood at the foot of the stairs with a camera, a cassette recorder, and a mischievous smirk. For us, the waiting was torture. But for my dad, a lifelong crusader against instant gratification, it was soulful pleasure.

Fifteen minutes earlier, I'd leaped from my bed, rousted my siblings, and not waiting to see if they were following, raced into my parents' bedroom. I jumped in bed and shook my parents by their legs to wake them as I shouted the question to which I already knew the answer: "Can we go downstairs? Can we? Can we?"

My dad laughed. "Wait on the stairs," he said.

"But, Daaaaaad," we whined in unison.

He just shrugged his shoulders. Defeated, we marched to our spot on a stair just high enough to keep the tree out of view. Just like we did every year. It was an infuriating tradition. We'd waited for weeks—and now we had to wait some more.

The Christmas morning routine was (allegedly) born of my parents' desire to snap a few pictures of the children before the chaos of Christmas morning ensued—the photographic equivalent of notches on the wall to chart our growth. They took the photo every year, without exception. But whatever their ostensible motive, we were convinced that the real reason we waited was for my father's twisted pleasure. He wore a look of supreme self-satisfaction as, between pictures, he thrust an audio recorder in our faces to capture our impatient answers to his aggravating questions.

"We're going to go downstairs in a minute," he said that morning, in a serious, reportorial tone. "But *before* we go down, I'd like you to tell me what you think you're going to get for Christmas today."

"I hope I get the whole set of basketball cards," I said, in a high-pitched voice with a strong upper-Midwest accent. (Think Alvin the Chipmunk as a character in *Fargo*.)

"I think I'm going to get a racetrack," Andy said, an octave higher. (Think Alvin the Chipmunk in *Fargo* after taking a hit from a helium balloon.) "And Julianna's getting a kitchen set and a Big Wheel."

"I really hope I get my dog," I added.

"Well, you're not getting a dog," my dad replied, apparently having consulted with Santa.

Disappointed, I jumped to the kind of exaggerated conclusion kids often come to: This was going to be the *worst* Christmas ever. But two minutes later, when we were released from the stairs and dashed to the fireplace to retrieve our stockings from the mantle, things began to turn around. "I got a sweatband! I got a sweatband," I shouted excitedly. "It's a headband!" Andy was similarly enthused. "Me, too! A headband!" he yelled. The two of us screamed like the teenage girls you see in old videos of Elvis concerts. About white headbands.

A few minutes later, I opened a package containing a series of

Alfred Hitchcock solve-your-own-mystery books. My mom tried explaining who Hitchcock was, but I rudely shushed her, pretending that I was—remember, I'm nine—well acquainted with his oeuvre. But the best gift that year was a new pair of moon boots. "They're big boots that keep your feet warm and you can run like crazy in 'em," I explained to my parents. "You can even play football in 'em." After trying them on, I announced, "Whoa! You feel like you're on the moon!"

And here I should say that this is *not* an airbrushed recollection drawn from memory. I have re-created the scene for you exactly as it transpired. Because my parents kept the tapes.

I found them this past summer in a denim cassette case hidden inside a beat-up gym bag stashed in the corner of a seldom-used closet. They'd been there for at least five years. I had promised to pass them along to my youngest brother, Dan, who had volunteered to transfer them to digital. But I'd forgotten to hand them off, and obviously, no one had missed them.

I took the case to Starbucks one morning, along with a hand-held Memorex tape player—the last one in stock at Best Buy. Two other stores I called no longer sold cassette players. My five-year-old was mystified by the device. I explained that it was sort of like an iPod before iPods were invented. "Are they from the dinosaur ages?" she asked innocently.

I popped "XMAS 1979" into the Memorex expecting to be entertained. And I wasn't disappointed: There was a heated debate between Andy and me about the relative merits of slippers versus moccasins. There was Julianna, just learning to talk, calling me "Feeb." There was me making fart noises into the microphone before my dad sighed, "Don't do things like that"—and abruptly turned off the recording.

I kept the tape rolling, only half paying attention, as I checked email and participated in a fantasy football mock draft. In the background, I could hear Andy making sound effects for his Matchbox car chases around the living room floor—*vrrrrr-rooooom, vrrrrroooooom* for the bad guys, *weeeee-eeeew, weeeee-eeeew* for the cops—as everyone else continued opening their presents. More packages, more celebrating.

And then something unexpected snapped my head back—a voice I hadn't heard in years. I closed my laptop and turned up the volume. "Hello, Smiley. Where'd you get that?" said the raspy, singsong voice. "What do you have there?" It was Pop, my grandpa. He died nearly twenty years ago.

Pop lived half a mile from the house I grew up in, and we were extraordinarily close. I think of him often but hadn't heard his voice since he passed away and could no longer call it to mind. It literally took my breath away. His recorded chatter was brief—less than a minute—and on the day it took place, probably unremarkable. The tape simply captured us greeting him as he walked through the front door, just as we'd always done. We took a break from opening presents as we rushed to show him our treasures.

He asked about the cars on Andy's racetrack. "What do they do—go underneath there to stop them?" he asked. "We'll have to read the directions." His warmth was there, even in that snippet, even through the garbled audio. *He* was there. I heard a little more small talk and then another click. That was all. Christmas morning was over. And there I was, a grown man sitting in a crowded coffee shop with tears streaming down my face, and not a bit embarrassed about it.

I rewound the tape and listened to every sound again, from the beginning—the waiting, the needling, the cinnamon smell commentary, the voices squeaking, the paper ripping, the

Matchbox cars zooming, my grandparents arriving, even the fart noises.

There was nothing particularly memorable about the Christmas of 1979—I'd long forgotten the details of that morning. I got lots of presents I hadn't asked for and I didn't get the thing I wanted most. On a second listen, though, what stood out to me wasn't the exhilaration of the kids, but the enthusiasm of the adults. It certainly wasn't, as I'd first feared, the worst Christmas ever. And it probably wasn't the best Christmas ever. It was like all the Christmases that came before and like all the ones that followed.

❦

More than thirty years later, the technology had changed and I was playing a different role, but the tradition was the same. I stood at the bottom of the stairs holding a video recorder as my children waited, antsy, on the edge of the top steps. After some still photos, brief interviews, and a lot of whining ("But, Daaaaaad!"), I gave the word: "Alright."

Grace, eight years old, came first. "I'm leading the pack," she said as she tore down the stairs and zipped past the camera. The others—Conner, six, and Jane, almost three—followed just behind, working up to a full sprint by the time they traversed the foyer. Grace stopped abruptly as she crossed into the living room, nearly causing a wreck. She stood for a moment, mouth agape, saying nothing. The others did, too. Grace found her voice first.

"Whoa," she said slowly, inching forward into the dimly lit room. It was the kind of awe a grown-up might feel seeing the Grand Canyon, the Northern Lights, or Elle MacPherson. "What in the world did he *do*?" she asked in wonderment.

No doubt Santa deserved some credit. But so did my wife.

The room before them was a Christmas fantasyland, a picture of holiday magnificence, arresting in its creative splendor. The ornaments on the tree that we'd decorated weeks earlier sparkled under string after string of white lights. A platter of half-eaten cookies sat next to the fireplace, alongside a plate of mostly finished pepperoni pizza (left out because the Santa at our local mall had a sense of humor). Presents spilled from under the tree to the center of the room. A school of three fish—giant, helium-filled balloons, each four feet in length, with tails that propelled them forward—swam through the air. And thanks to a disco light that came with a new karaoke machine, the entire space was intermittently covered in flashes of green dots—sort of a sea-green if you were looking at the fish, Christmas green if your backdrop was the tree. It was mesmerizing.

I don't think my wife would object to me describing her as someone who gets a little carried away at Christmas. (We'll soon find out, I guess.) The scene was the result of weeks of effort and years of experience as a television producer. It was almost too glorious to disturb. Almost.

After the kids caught their breath, they charged into the room and grabbed the largest unwrapped gifts they could find. This year, that meant Paper Jamz guitars—fake guitars that come with three preprogrammed songs and small speakers that blare the music out of the front. The kids figured out how to work them at roughly the same time. Within moments, a predawn Christmas concert had begun at decibel levels so high that the sound would have filled a small arena. As it happened, each guitar played a different song, so we were treated to a medley, of sorts: Pat Benatar's "Hit Me with Your Best Shot," Steppenwolf's "Born to Be Wild," and "Elmo's World" (from the artist of the same name).

When the concert ended, Grace walked over to a tower of presents in white boxes and, pointing sequentially to each one, announced with pride to her mother that the pile was partly a product of her generosity. "This and this and this and this and this are from me . . . and Daddy."

"You guys are so generous," my wife replied, clearly moved. "You know what I like to see? Your face is just as excited about giving as it was about—"

"Awesome!!!!" Grace cut her off, pointing to the other side of the room, where she spied a blue platypus with a CD player for its rear end. "It's Perry the Platypus!"

It went on like this for most of the day, not because of the number of presents but because, after the opening rush, their package-opening rate slowed dramatically. They tried out each new gift for a while—sometimes playing with it for more than an hour—before turning to the next one. The pace allowed us to catch up on some of the sleep we'd missed the night before. My wife was up until nearly dawn putting together an elaborate medieval castle; I'd run to CVS at 2:30 a.m. to buy extra helium for the flying fish. This, after weeks of Christmas parties, holiday concerts, and frenzied last-minute shopping.

The kids unwrapped their packages and played with their toys and read their books. We opened gifts from the kids and each other and occasionally dozed off. There was orange juice and there were cinnamon rolls. It was just like the Christmases that came before and those that will follow.

Winter in the nation's capital is miserable after Christmas.

For two months, a blanket of cold, wet grayness covers the region, neither cold enough to produce a real winter nor warm enough to make being outdoors any fun. Average temperatures run to the low forties, so the beautiful white snowfalls of my youth in Wisconsin have given way to gloomy days of sleet and slush, euphemized by cheerful forecasters as a "wintry mix." Technically, the winters are shorter here. But they feel longer.

And so it was on January 14, 2015, as I trudged out the front door and into a cold, spitting rain. I left behind my wife and Jane, now a month shy of her fifth birthday. The plan for the morning, before afternoon preschool, was to strip the Christmas tree, bring down the lights, pack up the Nativity scene, throw out the wreath, and put everything away until next year.

When she saw what was happening, Jane objected, quietly at first, and eventually in a full-blown, top-of-her-lungs tirade. "Why, why, why?" she asked. "Why are you taking down Christmas? Why, why, why, why, why?!?! Don't you see this is frustrating to me?" She stomped her feet and clenched her fists. She was committed.

"Maybe you need a home day today, Jane," my wife said with the patience she always manages to find.

"What I need is for you to hear me! Stop undoing Christmas! Don't you support Santa? And baby Jesus? You're just going to take *Him* down? Stuff Him in a box? He gave us His life, Mom. *His life!*"

I wasn't there for the drama. But I was gratified that our emphasis on the Jesus in Christmas had stuck with her, and even prouder that she threw in a little Easter to try to keep her mother from undoing Christmas.

And she may be right. Perhaps the problem isn't that we have too much Christmas, but that we don't have enough.

The modern American Christmas is a process that unfolds over nearly one-fifth of the calendar year—from the time you see the first displays at Kmart in late October until you slide the final box of decorations back into its place in mid-January. Adults and children live this process in very different ways.

Kids spend the weeks leading up to Christmas taking part in a steady stream of activities designed to heighten their anticipation of Christmas Day; adults scramble to complete a long list of tasks before the big day finally arrives. Children count the days until Christmas morning; adults are panicked that it's coming so quickly. Kids go to bed early on Christmas Eve and, in their excitement, have a hard time falling asleep; adults push the boundaries of physical and mental endurance in their attempts to build elaborate toys or assemble remote-controlled robots. On Christmas morning, kids race around as if they've spent the night on sugar-water IVs, while the adults pound extra coffee just to stay conscious. Children attack wrapping paper and ribbons like lions slaughtering gazelles; adults prefer that kids open their packages in an orderly fashion, disposing of the waste as they go. After Christmas, excited kids embark on new adventures with their new toys; exhausted adults ask one another if they've "survived" Christmas.

Yet somehow, in my experience at least, adults look forward to Christmas with the same eagerness and excitement as their children. For kids, the wonder of Christmas is Santa Claus and impossible sleigh rides, unlikely chimney descents and flying reindeer, elaborately decorated trees, and of course, abundant gifts.

For adults, the wonder of Christmas is children.

CHAPTER 11

The Ghosts of Christmas

Holidays Past and Present

Toby Young

SHAME DESCENDED on the Young household last Christmas. When my wife, Caroline, picked up our nine-year-old son from school on the last day of the term, she was intercepted by his teacher, who wanted a quiet word.

Oh no, she thought. *What's Ludo done now?*

In fact, it was more a case of what I'd done—or failed to do. The teacher explained that she'd asked the children to write "letters to Santa," saying what they wanted for Christmas. At the top of his list Ludo had written: "Light bulb." When the teacher asked him why he'd chosen such an unusual present he told her that the bulb in his bedroom had stopped working six months ago. Ludo's hope was that if Santa put a bulb in his stocking, his deadbeat dad might finally get around to replacing it.

One of the reasons I was so embarrassed by this story is that, for years now, I've been complaining about how greedy my kids are when it comes to Christmas presents. Ludo has never asked for anything as modest as a light bulb before. On the contrary, he has presented me with endless lists, some stretching to several sides of foolscap, nearly all of which contain items like Xbox and PlayStation accompanied by detailed drawings. When he was four, he spent the best part of an afternoon drawing a picture of a "Roket" and then painstakingly explained that this rendering wasn't supposed to be actual size. He wanted a real rocket, one that could take him to the moon.

The sheer ambition of Ludo's requests is quite endearing. Clearly, he is still an innocent when it comes to money. Not so my daughter, who's two years older. Even as a five-year-old, she knew that if she asked for anything costing more than £25 she'd be unlikely to get it. Where she went wrong was in asking for more or less everything in this price bracket. She was so suggestible that she only had to see an advertisement for, say, Hot Wheels Shark Bite Bay, and she wanted it. And I mean, really, really wanted it, as in ran down to my garden office and told me she absolutely must have it. I often thank God that we're not yet in the era when you can purchase something advertised on television with one click of a button on the remote. If we were, the ground floor of our house would look like a Toys"R"Us warehouse.

Some parents don't allow their children to watch commercial television for precisely this reason, but I'm not sure whether that would make much difference. Mine would only get to hear about the same must-have toys on the playground. Two years ago, five-year-old Charlie announced he wanted a Nintendo DS for Christmas. Caroline asked if he knew what it was since he'd never shown any interest in video games before. "Of course I do," he said. "It's this really cool machine for making sweets." We managed to fob him off with a Pez Machine that year.

※

I'm a typically annoying father in that I agree beforehand that Caroline will be in charge of buying the children's presents, and after she's wrapped them up and attached labels saying they're from both of us, I then go out and buy additional gifts on Christmas Eve. I hand them over the following day, explaining that they're "special presents from Dad." Last year

I got Ludo a "Lollipop Factory," which went down like a cup of cold sick with Caroline. "There's nothing I hate more in the world than lollipops," she said.

The depressing thing about buying my children toys is how little pleasure they sometimes seem to get from them. On Christmas Day, they tear off the wrapping paper, glance at the present with barely concealed disappointment, and then immediately move on to the next one. There's something predatory about it, like velociraptors hunting for fresh meat.

Often, they have to be coaxed into playing with the toys I've bought them, even though they were begging for them just days before. This involves them opening the boxes, emptying their contents on to the carpet, and then mixing up all the little bits into a potpourri of multicolored plastic. After they've gone to bed, late on Christmas evening, I spend several hours on my hands and knees sifting through the pile, trying to put the right bits into the right boxes, like a low-level CIA grunt trying to piece together secret documents after they've been shredded. As a general rule, you lose about 10 percent of the detachable parts every time a toy is played with.

The worst offender in this respect is Playmobil. Last year, one of Ludo's godparents bought him the Playmobil Large Pirate Ship, a build-it-yourself scale model that consists of over one hundred separate parts. Within minutes of Ludo opening it, some of these bits had fallen through the floorboards and others had been kicked under the fridge, while still others had been snatched up by Charlie and added to his Lego collection. By the time Ludo and I had finished building it, even a bunch of Somali pirates would have turned up their noses at it.

To date, the most successful present I've ever bought Ludo is a Thomas the Tank Engine train set. While Magnetix and Moon Sand are still sitting in their boxes, having been played with once and forgotten, the train set is constantly being broken up and reassembled. Ludo has now lost interest in it, but eight-year-old Freddie has been gripped by Thomas mania, and in time I daresay Charlie will be, too. My only caveat is to advise against buying battery-operated engines. All three of my sons love nothing more than switching them on, leaving them on their side so the wheels spin around endlessly, and then abandoning them.

My three least favorite words at Christmastime are "batteries not included." I'm sure if I actually sat down and calculated my greatest expense each year, the spreadsheet would say: batteries. If I had half a brain I'd give up journalism entirely and start selling the damn things door to door. Earlier this year, we rented a cottage from a retired couple living very comfortably in Cornwall. As they were off to the local yacht club one day, pulling a sailboat behind a brand-new SUV, I asked them how they'd made their money. "Batteries," they said.

Christmastime was a very different affair when I was a boy. My father, Michael, was a big believer in Christmas. That is to say, he liked the idea of it. My older sister and I were the products of his second marriage—to our mother, Sasha—and he would usually invite the children from his first marriage to our house for lunch. It could be quite tense, with undercurrents of rivalry and resentment, but all the children made an effort to keep the atmosphere festive. We did this to protect our father's feelings. He was the opposite of a paterfamilias. His strategy for holding the family together was to cast himself as the weakest and most vulnerable member. His hope was that we'd pretend to get along in order to avoid upsetting him. And by and large we did.

Michael, who died in 2002, was a left-wing intellectual who helped set up a number of institutions that are now part of the fabric of British public life: the Open University, *Which* maga-

TOBY YOUNG ▪ 121

zine, and the University of the Third Age, among others. He was also a genuine eccentric. On the eve of a trip to Australia he once told me about a brilliant wheeze he'd come up with to minimize the amount of luggage he took with him. It involved wearing two of everything in transit. He proudly showed me how he'd prepared for the eighteen-hour flight by putting on two pairs of socks, two shirts, two suits, and so on.

Michael didn't simply want his children to come to Christmas lunch. He would also invite a variety of waifs and strays. For instance, there was Vincent Brome, an elderly literary gentleman in his nineties whose main topic of conversation was sex. He, at least, was a repeat guest. Quite often, the people seated around the table were complete strangers to us—and, indeed, to my father as well. He would disappear to his office in London's East End on Christmas morning, and if he spotted a tramp on his way back home at lunchtime he would bundle him into the car. It wasn't beyond him to turn up with two or three homeless people. He would give a great deal of thought as to where to place each guest at the table, making sure they were seated next to the person he thought they'd get on with best. He was the perfect host.

I remember one Christmas lunch being interrupted by a loud knocking at the door. It was the tramp who lived in the park across the street. As I was fishing in my pocket for a couple of quid, Michael appeared behind me and said, "Ah, Mr. Murphy, come in, come in. You're just in time."

This generosity didn't always go down well with my mum, who had to feed all these people, but she did her best. She only lost her temper with Michael once, and that was when he failed to show up for Christmas. We usually sat down to lunch at 2:00 p.m., but the hour came and went and there was no sign of him. We had a particularly fruity group of waifs and strays that year, and their only connection was that they had all been invited by my father. Without him there, the conversation didn't exactly flow. It was like the bar scene in *Star Wars*, rewritten by Harold Pinter.

Michael finally materialized at 4:30 p.m. and explained that he'd taken a detour via a cemetery in Bethnal Green, one of London's most deprived neighborhoods. He was generally fascinated by the subject of death—it was guaranteed to come up at every Christmas lunch—and he'd heard that on Christmas Day this particular cemetery was full of elderly, working-class women sharing "a cuppa" with their late husbands. The "sharing" consisted of pouring tea into their graves, while they updated them with all the latest family gossip.

Even when he turned up on time there was no guarantee we'd eat anything. I was about to tuck into my roast one Christmas when Mr. Murphy appeared at the door again. Michael immediately invited him to join us, but, having done so once, the gentleman wasn't inclined to repeat the experience. Instead, he asked if he could "borrow" five pounds, explaining that he'd been mugged earlier that day. It was obvious to everyone that this was just a ruse—everyone, that is, except my father. Like many liberals, his ability to see the best in people was allied to an essential innocence. However, instead of simply giving the homeless man a fiver, he rounded up a posse and insisted we go out and search for the thief. I spent the next hour patrolling the streets of Islington with my father, my half-brother, and the elderly Vincent Brome. Mr. Murphy trailed behind us at a distance, dumbfounded that his words had been taken at face value.

All this do-goodery makes my father sound a bit like Mrs. Jellyby, the "telescopic philanthropist" in *Bleak House* who places the interests of the poor and needy above those of her own family. There was certainly an element of that—nearly all high-minded socialists have a touch of Mrs. Jellyby about them—but his compassion was also rooted in experience. As a boy, he'd been neglected by his own parents, an Irish bohemian painter and a rackety Australian musician. It wasn't uncommon for his birthday to go completely unnoticed by them and on Christmas Day they often disappeared to the pub for hours, leaving him to fend for himself. Consequently, his heart always went out to those who were alone at Christmas—he didn't want them to feel unloved, as he had.

The reason he'd been so late the day he visited the cemetery is that he'd been so moved by the sight of these widows sitting by their husband's gravesides that he felt obliged to strike up conversations with them. Not surprisingly, they'd been eager to talk. And that's why he had difficulty getting away.

We had all been furious with him for keeping us waiting, but within fifteen minutes he managed to reduce us to tears, telling us about these wonderful, stoic characters, full of British pluck and able to laugh at their misfortune. We went from being angry that he was late to feeling ashamed that we'd put our own comfort and convenience before the needs of these heroic women. It was deeply manipulative, of course—suddenly, we were in the wrong!—but we didn't mind being manipulated by him. At some point during every Christmas lunch, my father would find a way to remind us of how lucky we were, usually by telling a story full of Dickensian pathos. It was part of the ritual.

As I watch my own children tearing through their piles of presents, I often reflect on how different their Christmas Days are from mine. My home is not a soup kitchen, and none of the local tramps would think to knock on my door for a bit of charity. Instead, it's just the usual round of eating, drinking, and rampant consumerism. My four children enjoy it and so do

I—I'm a capitalist, damn it—but I often think of my father and his unconventional attempts to spread a little Christmas cheer.

I miss him, obviously, and I also miss my half-siblings and Vincent Brome. More surprisingly, I miss the homeless men. Under my father's roof, Christmas was always a little strange and unsettling, but there was also something magical about it. Even though Michael wasn't a Christian, there was a connection with the tradition of sacrifice and generosity—of sharing your good fortune with others—that isn't much in evidence in my household.

Perhaps next year I'll take some time out on Christmas Day to visit his grave in Highgate Cemetery and share a cup of tea with him. Perhaps we'll talk about this.

CHAPTER 12

The War on Christmas
It's Real, and It's Spectacular

Jonah Goldberg

IN THE OPENING sequence of *Scrooged*—which Sonny Bunch correctly identifies as one of the great Christmas movies of the modern age—we're teased with the trailer for a movie called *The Night the Reindeer Died*. In this fictional made-for-TV movie, Santa's workshop is attacked by machine-gun-wielding terrorists. Amid heavy artillery fire, Mrs. Claus races to the gun locker to hand out heavy weapons to the elves. Suddenly, Lee Majors, the Six Million Dollar Man (that's $32 million in today's dollars), rides up on a snowmobile.

As the bullets fly, Majors asks Santa, "Is there a back way out of this place?"

Kris Kringle responds, "Of course there is, Lee, but this is one Santa who's going out the front door."

Majors nods silently in admiration of Santa's grit. But he warns St. Nick, "Look, it don't matter a hill of beans what happens to me, but the world couldn't afford it if anything happened to you. Now you stay put."

"Aw, that's very nice of you, Lee," Santa says gratefully. He then adds, "And, Lee, you're being a real good boy this year."

Majors then sets off on his death-dealing way to vanquish the enemies of Yuletide. "Eat this," he grunts as he mows down the Santa-sacking psychos with his modernized hand held Gatling gun.

Now that's my kind of war on Christmas.

Alas, today's "war on Christmas," which has become for cable news an annual ritual, is merely another one of those metaphorical wars, like the wars on women, poverty, cancer, global warming, history, energy, religion, and science. (I'm sure I'm leaving a few dozen out.)

Of course "metaphorical" doesn't mean "fictional." The "war" on poverty is—or was—a real thing; it just wasn't a *war.*

And yet the metaphorical wars have the capacity to elicit as much outrage as actual wars. For instance, in the Middle East and ever-growing swaths of Africa, there are nonmetaphorical wars on women, Christians, Jews, science, history, and gays. These wars have all the hallmarks of actual war, what with the killing, rape, and slavery. But in the United States the "war" on women that arouses so much passion from politicians and liberal activists should really be put in air quotes. Ditto the "war" on Christmas.

Of course, the left has always loved its metaphorical wars, ever since William James announced the pressing need for the "moral equivalent" of war. President Obama has kept that tradition alive, routinely calling for warlike unity in his effort to pour money down any number of rat holes. But the moment when the tail-chasing-dog ate himself came when Obama declared a lexicological war on war, changing the "war on terror" to "overseas contingency operations." Terrorist attacks became "man-caused disasters," and American reprisals were euphemized as "kinetic military operations." It was, to borrow a phrase, a metaphorical war to end all literal wars. We'll know that battle has been won when we start talking about the Domestic Contingency Operation against Christmas.

The merits of these metaphorical wars vary widely. War on cancer? Worth fighting. War on science? Mostly a bogus PR campaign to bully conservatives into silence. But the war on Christmas represents a special kind of passive-aggressive jack-assery because the aggressors deny they have declared a war. They simply take offense at Christmas cheer. They cancel Christmas pageants. They leave baby Jesus in a cardboard box in the church basement, but see nothing wrong with celebrating the Winter Solstice as if that's a more rational thing to do. And then, when people complain about this undeclared war on Christmas, the aggressors mock and ridicule them for paranoia and hyperbole.

Since we're comparing things to actual wars, it's a bit like Vladimir Putin's mischief in the Ukraine. He sends troops across the border, then denies they're Russian soldiers. The soldiers kill Ukrainians, but Russian TV floats the idea it's all a hoax trumped up by the West. Then, after the Russians create facts on the ground, they whine when anyone makes a fuss. So it is with the war on Christmas.

Before I continue, I should get some disclaimers out of the way. The war on Christmas is a fraught issue for a right-wing guy named Goldberg. So with some prodding from the spirit of Full Disclosures Past, let me disclose fully. I am Jewish, albeit with some considerable emphasis on the *ish*. My father insisted my brother and I be raised Jewish. I went to a Jewish day school and was duly bar mitzvahed, so please spare me long lectures on the matrilineal nature of Judaism.

In any event, my Episcopalian mother insisted we celebrate Christmas. So while many of my friends at school had "Hanuk-kah bushes" instead of Christmas trees, we had a Christmas tree with a single modification. My parents cut out a jokey headline from a local newspaper and taped it to a flat cardboard Christmas tree ornament. It read, "Santa Knows We're Jewish."

We have a similar policy in my own home. Every year we light the Hanukkah candles. And their glow has not once scared off Santa, who dutifully eats his cookies and leaves his presents.

So there's that. But the disclosures go on. I'm also a Fox News contributor (and happily so). Some of my colleagues—a generous term I use for people far more important and famous than yours truly—are generals in the War to Save Christmas. More on that in a bit.

Lastly, let me just say that I love Christmastime and I take no offense whatsoever when someone says to me, "Merry Christmas." Indeed, I think it is written somewhere in the Talmud that if you make someone feel bad for sincerely wishing you a "Merry Christmas!" it means you're a miserable, joyless ass (it sounds more high-minded in the original Hebrew). Of course, there's a flip side to that. If you know someone is not Christian or hates Christmas for some reason, and you say "Merry Christmas" out of spite or vindictiveness, rather than with joy and good cheer, then you are the one putting the "ass" in Christm*ass*.

And that is part of the genius of the left's passive-aggressive war on Christmas. By forcing Christmas-lovers—Christian and non-Christian alike—to take time out of their day to marshal a metaphorically martial defense of Christmas, they further undermine the whole point of the holiday, and the Holy Day. Turning Christmas into a battleground in the culture war compounds the damage they're already doing.

Which brings me to the story of Hanukkah, in a really forced and contrived kind of way. Alexander the Great (in Yiddish, "Alexander He Could Be Worse") conquered Palestine. But in the grand tradition of the "good czar," he left the Jews alone. A century later, Antiochus IV, the Greek king of the Seleucid Empire—and one of the great putzes of antiquity—reigned.

Except for the fact that Hanukkah didn't exist yet, you might say he declared a war on Hanukkah, by which I mean he set out to actually destroy the Jews who hadn't assimilated to Hellenistic culture. He appointed Greek priests to the High Temple, ordered the sacrifice of pigs on its altar, and killed Jews who wouldn't go along. The Jews revolted and threw off their oppressor. The Hanukkah candles we light every year do not commemorate that victory—Jews aren't supposed to glorify war—but rather the miracle of the untainted lantern oil lasting for eight nights in the temple, when there was only enough for one.

I bring this up because Jews have a lot of experience dealing with the challenges of living in societies where they are religious bystanders and nonconformists. From the dawn of the diaspora until 1948 (when Israel was founded), that was really their—our—*only* experience. And, to borrow a phrase from Jack Nicholson in *As Good as It Gets*, it wasn't all "pretty stories that take place at lakes with boats and friends and noodle salad." But it wasn't all bad either. One of the lessons Jews learned is that respect is a two-way street. In decent societies the majority shows respect to the minority. But part of the bargain is that minorities also show respect to the majority. This is supposed to be a fun book about a joyful time of year, so I will skip past more recent historical examples of what happens when this grand bargain goes ass-over-teakettle. Just take my word for it.

But the lesson is worth taking to heart when thinking about the war on Christmas. The conflict has never really been about Christmas. It's been about how a society tolerates conflicting visions of what kind of society people want.

The war on Christmas can best be understood as the point at which several tectonic plates of the culture grind together.

When they grind together really hard, we get earthquakes. The plates have been grinding together for generations, and they go by many names: secular humanism, nihilism, relativism, progressivism, Cthulhu, and others. The opposing forces have a lot of monikers as well: traditionalism, Christianity, conservatism, and, my favorite, the Good Guys. Christmas just happens to be one of the places where the Good Guys and Cthulhu fight on ground really favorable to the Good Guys.

That's because, properly speaking, Christmas should be about as controversial as puppies, kittens, motherhood, and Scotch: Just one of those things everyone agrees is a good thing. Indeed, that's the underlying assumption among Christmas' cable show champions: *Christmas used to be something that united us—but not anymore, thanks to the secular humanists, multicultural-ists, and other killjoys.* And that's absolutely true. Christmas *was* uncontroversial for a while. Then it was controversial. Then it was uncontroversial. And so on. That's because Christmas is in fact older than cable TV.

There's no mention of Jesus' birthday in the Bible. Indeed, for Christianity's first few centuries it was a nonissue (perhaps because when the Romans are feeding you to lions, figuring out Jesus' birthday is a relatively low priority). Death, specifically Jesus' death, was a much bigger deal theologically. In fact, early Christian writers mocked the Romans for their pagan habit of celebrating birth anniversaries.

Jesus' birthday only became a priority for the Church when people started to believe he wasn't a real person but a spirit or some such, according to the aforementioned Christmas scholar, Stephen Nissenbaum. Real humans are born, not invented (Al Gore notwithstanding). The Church reckoned that celebrating Jesus' birth would be a good way to under-line the fact that he was born flesh and blood. "If you want to show that Jesus was a real human being just like every other human being," Nissenbaum explained, "not just somebody who appeared like a hologram, then what better way to think of him being born in a normal, humble human way than to celebrate his birth?" The iconic crèche and manger scenes so associated with Christmas didn't become commonplace until the thirteenth century.

As for December 25, the Internet, among other sources, tells me in a fairly unified voice that the date was picked because it aligned with numerous pagan holidays associated with the Winter Solstice. We've all heard these theories before, and while scholars can debate around the edges, it doesn't seem like anyone truly disputes the notion that Christmas co-opted a whole lot of Germanic and Nordic traditions. The iconic Santa is more inspired by Odin than the Turkish St. Nicholas, and the Christmas tree has its historical roots in the Saturnalian practice of bringing holly into the home.

Still, long after Christianity had routed the pagans, Christmas remained controversial. The Puritans had huge problems with it. Because the holiday takes place in winter, when there's not much for farmers to do, it became a kind of spring break in the sixteenth and seventeenth centuries. In England, a country with a long and honorable tradition of looking for reasons to get drunk, the twelve days of Christmas became the kind of bacchanalia that would have made a great backdrop for a *Damsels Gone Wild* video series. Philip Stubbes, a sixteenth-century Jerry Falwell, decried this hedonism in his pamphlet *The Anatomie of Abuses*:

> That more mischief is that time committed than in all the year besides, what masking and mumming, whereby robbery whoredom, murder and what not is committed? What dicing and carding, what eating and drinking, what banqueting and feasting is then used, more than in all the year besides, to the great dishonour of God and impoverishing of the realm.

That wasn't the only problem with Christmas. Protestants didn't like the way Catholics observed the holiday, and vice versa. In England, the extravagant Christmas parties thrown by Catholics were seen, as P. J. mentioned, as uncouth, the "trappings of popery" and "rags of the beast" (two fantastic names for an ultramontane punk rock band). The Catholic Church tried to counteract the problem by emphasizing that Christmastime was a holy celebration, not an excuse to let your freak flag fly. But it ultimately didn't work. When Cromwell took over, he banned the holiday entirely, something the ACLU only dreams of doing today.

Cromwell's ban was lifted, but for a long time the popularity of Christmas dwindled in the New World and Britain. By 1820 the English poet and essayist Leigh Hunt wrote that it was a holiday "scarcely worth mention." It wasn't quite as forgettable as Arbor Day or the WNBA championships, but it wasn't the big deal we think of today, either. And the person most responsible for reviving it wasn't a religious figure at all, but a literary one: Charles Dickens.

Published in 1843, Dickens' *A Christmas Carol* was a staggering literary success—bigger than *Fifty Shades of Grey* and *The Dadly Virtues* combined. By Christmas of 1844, there were no fewer than nine stage productions of it in London. It was a huge sensation that year in New York as well. It popularized the salutation "Merry Christmas." One critic proclaimed, "If Christmas, with its ancient and hospitable customs, its social and charitable observances, were ever in danger of decay, this is the book that would give them a new lease. The very name of the author predisposes one to the kindlier feelings; and a peep at the Frontispiece sets the animal spirits capering."

There's a fascinating debate about how religious *A Christmas Carol* really is. There are a great many subtle scriptural allusions in the book that are lost on most people, including me; I wouldn't have caught many of them were it not for Stephen Skelton's annotated version of the story. On the other hand, while Dickens was a faithful Christian, the story is deeply ecumenical, even secular.

The key to the novella's appeal was its overpowering sense of nostalgia. "In fighting for Christmas," G. K. Chesterton observed, Dickens "was fighting for the old European festival, Pagan and Christian, for that trinity of eating, drinking, and praying which to moderns appears irreverent, for the holy day which is really a holiday." But it went deeper than that. Dickens had a famously rough childhood, and his stories were often child-centric. And so was his idea of Christmas.

Until *A Christmas Carol*, Christmas was more of a community celebration, a time for revelry. It was a lot like what New Year's Eve is today. But Dickens carved out Christmas as a special time for children. In the tale, the Ghost of Christmas Past takes Scrooge to his own childhood, where he sees himself abandoned as all the other kids have gone home to be with their families. "The school is not quite deserted," the Ghost observes. "A solitary child, neglected by his friends, is left there still." Scrooge sobs at the sight. The Ghost then takes poor Ebenezer to see children playing and making merry with their family. Scrooge exclaims, "What would I not have given to be one of them!" (As Rob Long—someone well acquainted with social ostracism and undesired solitude—points out, it would have been nice if someone, somewhere, had given *him* a giant turkey.)

Thanks to Charles Dickens, Christmas became a time when parents thought about the Christmas they wished they had had when they were kids. And so they set out to deliver it to their own children. That's one of the keys to Christmas' enduring popularity. As Bill Murray says in *Scrooged* (you knew I'd come back to that), at Christmastime, however briefly, "We are the people we always hoped we would be."

I am not Christian, but some of my favorite people are (including, among others, my wife, my mother, most of my coworkers and friends, and nearly all of my favorite presidents).

I have no objection to Christians seeking to keep the "Christ in Christmas." But it seems to me that the war on Christmas has less to do with a desire to keep the holiday somberly sacred and more to do with maintaining an idea of "America, the Way It Used to Be."

As a conservative, I get that. And it is absolutely true that the people who bang their hemp spoons on their high chairs at "Merry Christmas," get their dresses over their heads about Nativity scenes, or who think Santa is scarier than Satan—or even the Koch brothers—tend to be humorless prigs.

I'm not normally in the habit of giving advice to Christians about how to observe their faith. But as a tactical matter, if you want to put the Christ back in Christmas, my advice would be to follow Jesus' exhortation to turn the other cheek. The best offense against humorless prigs isn't counterveiling humorless priggery. It's good cheer. If someone gets angry when you say, "Merry Christmas!" chuckle and tell them, "For your sake, I won't tell Santa about this."

And take comfort in the knowledge that the Christmas haters are not merely losers, they are losing. Most Americans—who spend almost a trillion dollars a year at Christmastime by the way—understand those people are idiots. If anything, Christmas keeps winning in the war on Christmas because Christmas is so much Odin-damn fun! So enjoy the holiday on Dickensian grounds—faith, family, fun all mixed into one. Say "Merry Christmas" with joy in your heart and have a good time—if for no other reason than the fact that nothing pisses off the people who hate Christmas more than people actually enjoying Christmas.

And by all means, let us redouble our efforts in our defensive war against relativism or the relentless erosion of our culture by political correctness. But there are other days of the year to have those arguments. The whole point of Christmas *is not to have arguments.* That's what Thanksgiving dinner is for.

CHAPTER 13

Jews Who Love Christmas
We All Love Christmas Magic

Larry Miller

WAIT, WHAT? Jews love Christmas? This one does. Why? Let's start here:

"Chestnuts roasting on an open—"

No, no, no, don't just skim through it the way you were going to. Read it slowly with a smile. You know it'll make you happy. I'll start again.

Chestnuts roasting on an open fire
Jack Frost nipping at your nose
Yuletide—

I'll bet you fifty cents you sang the whole thing through just three words in, because this is one of the greatest Christmas songs of all time, music and words by Mel Tormé and Robert Wills. It's lovely, and the lyrics are charming.

That's a very big part, you know, the words. If you read those words without smiling, you not only don't love Christmas, you don't like hot cocoa, you don't like snowball fights, you don't like pie. Hell, you probably don't like breasts.

But that's not why I love Christmas.

Let's start further back with the Christmas lights. Yay! Hanging big, colorful lights (not those goofy, new white ones) is the most fun you could ever—

Oh, wait, no it's not. The kids were going to help you, but that only lasted two minutes before they ran back inside to play their *Kill Everyone* video game, and your wife couldn't stand to watch you do it alone and pretend you were rugged. You mashed your thumb with the hammer so many times you actually called out the name of the guy you were supposed to be celebrating. Hmm. There's got to be another way. . .

Reading to the kids from the Bible! That's the ticket! Okay, you couldn't find anything appropriate right away, and you don't know much about the Bible anyway, and the kids were thinking of selling you to Gomorrah, so your wife sent them back to the living room to play their other favorite video game, *Death! Death! Death!*

Ooh, here's the best place to start, right on the bull's-eye: Christmas Day!

The joy of children running downstairs in their pajamas is the greatest gift Mom and Dad could ever want. Your arm may be around your wife's shoulder as you watch them open their gifts, but neither of you is saying anything, because the lumps in your throats are too big.

The day keeps getting better. You and the family stop into a couple of friends' houses, and the laughter is sweet. "Merry Christmas!" "Merry Christmas!" It's brief, though, because you have a destination, and you pile in the car and drive to Aunt Marion and Uncle Milton's house, and all your siblings and cousins and kids and grandparents are there, and the hugs and kisses and compliments are like bags of treasure.

Grandma is ninety-two, but she has never looked happier, and the drinks and toasts are fabulous—especially the second one!

The dining room, though, oh, that dining room. It's simple

but full of pictures and lace, and there's never been a more beautifully set table. Your cousin Harry is back from Afghanistan and wearing his dress uniform with a new medal, and everyone has hugged and kissed him again and again. He was wounded on a difficult mission, but recovered fully, and he asks to say grace, and it's so moving there isn't a dry eye in the house, including yours.

That's the perfect time to eat! Uncle Milton carries the turkey in and starts to carve at the head of the table, but before he does, he looks around and says, "Merry Christmas." You look around, too, and return all the smiles and nods, and the colorful sweaters and sport coats and dresses make you think no family has ever been this lovely.

Snow falls gently on the ride home, it's quiet and sleepy, and you find yourself humming, "The first Noel, the angels did sing . . ." Christmas is the best day of the year.

With one tiny problem. It never happened.

What?

You heard me. That dinner never happened. Not to you, not to anyone. Christmas Days like that never occur in real life, and you know it. They only happen in movies written by Jews who love Christmas.

But that's not why I love Christmas.

❧❀❧

Come on, folks. Your kids weren't giggling when they opened their gifts in the morning, because you didn't get them what they wanted. Giggling? Heck, there was yelling. Your wife is mad, because she tells you she hates flowers every time you get them for her, and you just can't think of anything else under the pressure and always get her flowers again the next time. The dog sees the tree every year and uses it the way dogs use trees, again and again, and who do you think is assigned to clean that up? Also, you had a *little* too much to drink last night, and when you made your big romantic move she decided to watch TV in bed—alone *with her flowers.* You hate—that's right, HATE—buying gifts for everyone and spending so much money and never making anyone happy. Sure, all your relatives had big smiles when you got there, but they were cranky inside, because now they and you have to figure out when to remove the explosively flammable trees in all your homes and the thousands of stupid Christmas lights no one wanted to put up in the first place and no one wants to take down. Everyone left the party early, because no one could stand being together anymore, and they all wanted to get home and drink heavily to forget this idiocy, and Aunt Marion and Uncle Milton were the angriest of all, because they had to clean all the kids' crapola off their furniture. Your sister suggested everyone sing a song before leaving, and one of her kids actually said, "Oh, shut up." The only reason your ride home was quiet was because as soon as you started the engine, you and your wife and kids sighed and shouted in unison, "God, I hate our family."

That one sound more familiar? It's easy for Jews to love this, because we don't have to do it. We catch the grim looks at work, though, like somehow it's still our fault.

That's actually the big problem. I don't know if you've noticed, but the last two thousand years have seen some chair-flying bar fights between Christians and Jews. Christians kill the Jews and burn their temples and rob every deli, and then, wouldn't you know it, the Jews turn right around and—

Okay, maybe the Jews don't do anything at all except try to tip-toe away, but there's a lot of anger out there, and pickle-heads in Domed Corporations are always drawing up plans to make things better. (For instance, a couple of years ago a national fast-food chain came up with a new breakfast item: ham and cheese on a bagel. I swear, I still don't know whether that's a giant leap forward or the dumbest thing I've ever heard.)

In Hollywood, where I work, gorgeous actresses marry Jewish producers all the time. You know this.

The actresses are from Nebraska—blonde, beautiful, twenty-six, and with names like Constance Collier. The men are from a long line of furniture salesmen on Long Island, eighty pounds overweight, bald, bearded, almost fifty, and named Ira Fingerhut. Their children are easy to pick out in private schools by the perfect mixture of Zero Mostel and Grace Kelly on their faces and their permanent inability to ever stop saying, "Okay, I have no idea what's going on." In other words, there is a great deal of confusion at this particular intersection.

✳✳✳

But it can all be fixed. Let's start from the beginning.

Question: What is Christmas?

Answer: The birthday of a Jewish man.

Ironic, no? He was a carpenter, sure, we all say that, but it means nothing to what he became and what he is. Maybe it will be the first time for you, but please listen to this carefully:

Jesus was a Jew, a real Jew, a full Jew, a complete Jew, a committed Jew, 100 percent Jew, a rabbi, in fact. There were no Christians in his life, none, because there were no Christians anywhere until *after* his life. Jesus was born a Jew, lived as a Jew, prayed as a Jew, preached as a Jew, died as a Jew, and loved God as a Jew. The first ten thousand Christians were *Jews*. Your ancestors were still huddled in caves in Scotland. They had thick hair and blue eyes and no idea who the Romans were.

We don't know what Mary and Joseph looked like, but it's a cinch they looked a lot more like Elliot Gould and Lainie Kazan than Brad Pitt and Gwyneth Paltrow.

The Apostles? Jews. Pontius Pilate? Roman. The audience at the Sermon on the Mount? Jews. The guests at Pilate's parties? Romans. Mary Magdalene? A Jew. Marching soldiers who were great at torture? Romans. Likable people in the New Testament? Jews.

But that's not why I love Christmas.

I had a great Christmas, once. That's right, wise guys, I did.

One of my best friends in college invited me to his home for Christmas. They lived in New Hampshire and his parents were fine people. He had a bunch of brothers and sisters, and they all lived in an old, rambling wood house that was big and strong. My friend, Jeff, knew I had never seen a Christmas, and his parents invited me. I asked my folks, and they said, "Sure, go and have fun. Just make sure you don't sign anything." (Kidding.)

So I went with Jeff to New Hampshire for a few days and had a real storybook event. They weren't doing anything extra, but the lights and the tree and the snow and the outfits (they lent me a sweater with Santa on it) were a pleasure.

I was staying in one of their extra bedrooms on the top floor, and that high, wooden, puffy bed was great. I remember the floor had a small grate in it from the basement where the heater was. Can you imagine? A house so old it had grates for heat. The kids all went to sleep Christmas Eve just like the song: "Tiny tots with their eyes all aglow."

All the kids woke me up giggling Christmas morning, which was very sweet, because they did it before running downstairs to their gifts. I had gotten a few gifts for them from a local store the day before with Jeff, and you know what? They got me one, too! It was under the tree with my name on it and hand wrapped, and that may not sound like much to you, but I almost cried. It was so nice of them to invite me and get me something, and I sat under the tree in my pajamas and slippers, just like them.

We had a big, farm breakfast, and I politely didn't eat some of the extravagantly nonkosher things, because it's unsettling to stare down the table at a platter with the whole face of the pig on it. (Still kidding.) We spent the day together and made a snowman. They had an organ, and we sang songs.

In the afternoon we got in their station wagon (that's right, a *station wagon*), the kids in the back, and went to a few of their friends' homes, with big "Merry Christmas!" shouts walking in. Their friends' homes were just right, too, and the laughs and stories and smiles were also just right. And I was one of those who was smiling.

The snow on the ride home was gentle, and the sleep that night was extra good. And the best part? This is all true. I was living in a Norman Rockwell painting for three days, and I was part of a good family, and for the first time, well, I could see why people loved Christmas.

Please understand the most important thing is that it ended. Let's be clear on that. This was a great chance to be with my friend and his family. It wasn't a training program; it was a gift, a visit, a glimpse. It's like seeing Belgium. Unless you're a lunatic, once is enough. It's your holiday, not mine.

But that's not why I love Christmas either.

It's time to tell you why, and I think you'll know just what I mean.

Back out in New Jersey, where my sister and her family used to live, there was a family a few blocks away. Camuso was their name. Ernest Camuso, the husband and father, was born in Newark, served in World War II, and moved to Livingston in 1949, where he lived for the rest of his life. He got married, had kids, and started working for the Lionel Company—God, how I loved their trains!—and then he opened his own business making all sorts of plastic molded goods. He was great with his hands, and the business was successful, and he supported his family well.

Ernest had a hobby that became a passion. He decorated his house and his front lawn for Christmas every year for fifty years. You're probably thinking, *What's the big deal? Lots of people do that.* Not like this they don't. Not like Ernest Camuso. It's like the difference between a garden hose and Niagara Falls. I was there once, then twice, then many times, and it was so good I would stand there looking for an hour and walk back to my sister's smiling, and they were smiling, too.

What did he put there? What *didn't* he put there? There was Santa and his sleigh and birds and angels and so many lights, just the right way, hundreds, thousands, a powerful statement in bold colors. There were paths and candy and characters and scenes, so much Christmas gear you'd think you had walked into a warehouse.

Too much? Past that. Way too much. Salesmen for this stuff would have said, "Maybe you should cut back." Plus, he wasn't limited by Christmas. He loved Disney characters, so he put out Snow White and the Dwarves, and Mickey and Minnie—I can't even list how many things. It was like the Sistine Chapel: You have to see it to believe it.

And right in the middle of it all was his Christmas tree. And what a tree it was. Thirty feet tall, *thirty feet,* lit like the angels made it, every inch decorated, and it was there every year. It really was, because it wasn't real, it was made by him, with an old washing machine as its core.

Every item was one too many. How could it ever work? It couldn't.

But here's the magic: It did work! Ernest made it work. It was fabulous. It was hypnotic. It was better than anything you've ever seen. It was . . . perfect.

Just a regular house with a regular lawn, but the Christmas

show was *so* big, and *so* much, and *so* far over the top, but never too big, or too much, or too far over the top. How did the neighbors feel? They loved it every year. The block loved it, the neighborhood loved it, the whole city, the whole state. Then much more. Thousands and thousands of people looked forward to it every year.

Families drove from several states away to see it, and I'm not kidding. That's how I got there. Every year my sister would say, "You've got to come see it. Please come out. Tomorrow." Finally, one year when I was home from school on Christmas break, my parents and I went. We drove from Long Island one morning, picked up my Uncle Arnie in Brooklyn, and headed to Livingston, New Jersey.

We have a very close and loud family and had a good, big meal together, followed by our traditional *huge* argument with no affection at all and plenty of snarling, and then, instead of watching television, or having another big argument (which would have been *easy*), we all put on our scarves and coats and walked through a couple of backyards and a few bushes on our first trip to Camuso Land.

We never had to be talked into it again. Oh, folks. My parents and I stood in front of the Camuso's white picket fence and took it in for two hours. Then we smiled at each other and smiled at my sister and smiled at all the cars going by. Then we all walked back through the bushes to her house.

One of Ernest's kids, Susan, recalled in an interview that they turned everything off at midnight, but at two or three in the morning, families would knock on their door and say, "Ooh, my cousins drove from Vermont and just got here. Could you please turn it on for just another minute?"

Ernest Camuso died a few years ago and joined his wife in heaven—and my parents, too—and his kids put all the Christmas things in the basement and the garage and the back room, and didn't know what to do, and time went by. It was all over.

Then one of their neighbors came by one day in the spring and asked if she could buy a couple of things from it, an angel or a reindeer or a train, and Susan thought, *It just doesn't seem right to give it away piece by piece.*

Then a few more people asked, and the kids thought they might try to put it up again, but lots of the parts were cracked and damaged and dirty. Then others from Livingston called and asked if they could help. It meant a lot to them for many years, and they didn't want it to vanish.

Then someone from the local government called and said he heard about it . . .

It turns out it wasn't all over. It wasn't all over at all.

Today, folks, at Christmastime, the city of Livingston puts up Ernest Camuso's Christmas show on a public piece of land and gives the family a big basement room at City Hall that they use to fix everything. A local fireman donates his time to paint Mickey and Minnie and everything else that needs it, and many others pitch in to keep it all working, too. They're all going to be there a long time, and they're all pleased as punch.

If I can get my family back there, I'm going to take them, too. One of my sons is a Marine, and I think him standing tall in front of that tree will please Ernest and his wife, and maybe just get a smile from God on down through everyone up there.

Isn't that something? A celebration of this and that, Ernest lives on, and his Christmas does, too, with many elves fixing it in their workshop.

And *that's* why I love Christmas.

One wonderful man and his family can save the heart and soul of it—and remember that it needs to be topped by a cross—and thousands of people are so touched for fifty years they join a team to keep it going.

If all you folks can keep it going, too, that'd be all right with me. It's not my holiday, but I'll be standing there smiling. Remember, we're closer than you think. Listen:

- "Rudolph the red-nosed reindeer had a very shiny nose."
- "I'm dreaming of a white Christmas."
- "Let it snow, let it snow, let it snow!"
- "Chestnuts roasting on an open fire."
- "Walking in a winter wonderland."
- "It's the most wonderful time of the year."
- "Silver bells, silver bells, it's Christmastime in the city."
- "I'll be home for Christmas."

Every note and word written by Johnny Marks, Irving Berlin, Sammy Cahn and Jule Styne, Mel Tormé and Robert Wills, Felix Bernard, George Wyle and Edward Pola, Jay Livingston and Ray Evans, Walter Kent and Samuel Ram. All great pros, all successful artists—

Oh, yes, and one more thing: All Jews.

Ah, well. Where did the day go? Time to move on to other things. But for now, here's part of a song I sang every year in elementary school. I loved it then, and still have no idea what it means:

Here we come a-wassailing among the leaves so green!
Here we come a-wand'ring, so fair to be seen!

Love and joy come to you,
And to you your wassail, too.
And God bless you and send you a Happy New Year,
And God send you a Happy New Year!

CHAPTER 14

I'm Dreaming of a Jewish Christmas

Celebrating a Day You Don't Really Share

Joseph Epstein

THE FIRST OF the few fights I ever had with my father was over a Christmas tree. I was five or six years old, and he and I were returning from the 400 Theatre on Sheridan Road in Chicago where we had seen a movie—I cannot recall its title—that had to do with Christmas. Walking the four or so blocks home, I asked my father if we couldn't have a Christmas tree. I didn't imagine getting one might be a problem. In my memory our conversation went roughly like this:

"That's not possible," he said.

"Why not?" I asked.

"Because we are Jews," he said, "and Christmas is about the birthday of Jesus Christ in whom we Jews do not believe."

"Why do we need to believe in him to get a tree?" I asked.

I call this a fight, but it was no match, for I lost on a TKO in the first round.

"All I want is a tree," I said.

"Jews don't have Christmas trees," he said. "I don't want to hear anything more about it."

"That's unfair," I said. Kids, then and now and always, are great collectors of injustice, and I was no exception.

"Unfairness has nothing to do with it. Discussion ends here."

I remember walking the rest of the way home in silence, sulking, unable to grasp my father's unreasonableness, when he was always so generous and reasonable about everything else.

Years later my father told me that on Christmas Eve, when he was five years old, he put his long white stockings—boys in those days wore knickers, requiring long stockings—on the mantle of his family's apartment in Montreal and woke the next morning to discover that one of his six older brothers had filled them with coal.

Before going further, I ought to make plain that my father wasn't in the least observant of Jewish ritual. This despite the fact that his father was a Jewish *erudit*, a man who obeyed all the dietary laws of *Kashrut* (or kosher) and prayed with regularity, each morning strapping on his phylacteries, as on various occasions I watched him do when he visited us in Chicago. I don't know what my grandfather thought of his son's want of Jewish observance, which extended to our never having belonged to a synagogue in all the years I lived at home—though my brother and I were bar mitzvahed and pork was never served in our house.

Later in life my father declared himself, on religious questions, an agnostic; on brave days, he announced himself an atheist. On the large questions he never referred to God but supplanted God with Nature. Only Jews, I suspect, can be both atheists and yet so intensely Jewish on all questions that do not touch directly on God. My father was one of these. God apart, he was chauvinistically, one might almost say relentlessly, Jewish. He gave large sums to Israel and to Jewish charities: the Anti-Defamation League, the Jewish United Fund, Hadassah, B'nai B'rith, *et alia*.

Unobservant in his own life, he nonetheless required, without being tyrannical about it, that his two sons go to Hebrew school four afternoons a week, that they have rabbinically officiated circumcisions for their own male children, and that they themselves remain stalwart in their pride in being Jews. He was always on the *qui vive* for anti-Semitism. "Some people may just hate you for your name," he told me when I was ten or eleven. The notion of avoiding this by changing one's name was beyond unthinkable. Jewishness was a club from which, after all that had happened in Europe, it would be a disgrace to resign. The club, as he often pointed out, also happened to be filled with an inordinately large proportion of people of extraordinary achievements, and the Jews themselves had survived against momentous odds.

The problem for me as a kid was that Christmas didn't seem so much a Christian as an American holiday, perhaps *the* American holiday. And to be excluded from it made me feel, somehow, less than fully American. As for Christianity, in those days and perhaps until I was ten or so years old, I thought Christianity and Catholicism were coterminous. This was in good part owing to the neighborhood in which we lived, Rogers Park, where most of the not obviously Jewish kids on our large block went to St. Jerome's and then on either to St. George or St. Scholastica high schools.

Chicago in those days was a very Catholic city. Ask someone where he lived, and he was likely to mention his parish: St. Nicholas, St. Rita, or St. Leo. (Non-Catholics would mention the nearest public park: Chase, Indian Boundary, or Green Briar.) Priests and nuns were plentiful in those days—the 1940s and early 1950s—and taught in the Catholic schools. Priests in collar and nuns in habit walked the streets; rode the buses, Els, and streetcars; and were part of the urban landscape. As a seven- or eight-year-old boy, I can remember, on the Sheridan Road bus, asking, "Sister, would you like my seat?" Or saying, in unconscious imitation of Barry Fitzgerald, "Morning to you, Father."

I mention Barry Fitzgerald because he played a priest in some of the popular movies of my moviegoing boyhood years. Generally, movies during those years seemed dominated by priestly stories. There was *Going My Way* (1944) and *The Bells of St. Mary's* (1945), in both of which Bing Crosby played a priest. Earlier there was *Boys Town*, with Spencer Tracy straightening out the intransigent Mickey Rooney. In a great many movies the actor Pat O'Brien, in the part of a priest, seemed to be walking killers down the last mile to the electric chair before they offered him a bawling confession. In 1947 there was *Miracle on 34th Street*. In 1954 Crosby returned, this time in mufti, in *White Christmas*. In 1959 Audrey Hepburn turned up in *The Nun's Story*. The movie *It's a Wonderful Life* (1946) is properly described as a Christmas fantasy. One couldn't, in those days, go to the movies without Christmas turning up, with large Christmas trees in supporting roles.

In the building just to the north of ours on Sheridan Road lived the Cowlings. I have heard a stray psychological theory— it's closer to a notion—that at some point in their lives all children believe, however briefly, that their parents cannot be their true parents. What they believe instead is that, if they are not in fact royalty, they are surely higher born than to the rather ordinary people with whom they have been assigned to live. I don't give this theory much credence, but I do know that, at age nine, if I had been asked to trade my parents for Sam and Dale Cowling I would have done so without the least hesitation, or stipulation of a kindly uncle-to-be-named-later.

Sam Cowling, the father, was a comedian, and appeared every morning on a then nationally famous show called *Don*

McNeill's The Breakfast Club, which ran for more than thirty-five years on ABC radio. He did a regular bit, announced with great fanfare, called "Fiction and Fact and Sam's Almanac." A small man, stocky and handsome, he was kind to everyone and played softball on Sundays in the fields behind our buildings along the lake. Dale Cowling was beautiful, in a motherly way; the very name Dale was pleasing—the name, it will be recalled, of Roy Rogers' wife. The Cowlings' two sons, Sammy and Billy, were blondish and crew-cutted, and both came to be good basketball players. The boys went to Chicago Catholic schools and then, I believe, to Georgetown. The Cowlings had a Christmas tree that took up a good part of their living room. One year all the lights on the tree were blue. They were a wonderful family and couldn't have been less Jewish, or should I say more *goyesque?*

Although Jewish kids may have predominated, if very slightly, in the two grammar schools I went to—Eugene Field on Lunt Avenue, and later Daniel Boone on Washtenaw Avenue—the understanding was that the country was Christian, and Christmas carols—"Silent Night," "Oh, Tannenbaum," "The Little Drummer Boy"—were sung without any of the Jewish kids asking to be excused. Some did irreverent Jewish parodies of these songs outside school—"Deck the halls with *schmaltz* and *cholly*"—but there wasn't the least bad feeling that we had Christianity, by way of music, imposed on us.

I wonder if Christmas carols are sung in public schools today, without giving equal time to Hanukkah, Kwanzaa, and other ethnic seasonal songs? I hope they are. I know as a boy, I never felt in the least offended by singing Christmas carols. Music is, after all, the great Christian art, surpassing, in my view, its painting and literature. (One thinks of Mozart's *Requiem* and the many Bach chorales and cantatas.) Not carols but two of the most popular Christmas songs were, of course, written by Jews: "White Christmas" by Irving Berlin and "The Christmas Song (Chestnuts Roasting on an Open Fire)" by Mel Tormé. I only regret that Cole Porter didn't write a song about Simchat Torah and Johnny Mercer about Purim.

Jews, until the founding of Israel in 1948, have always been strangers in others' lands, and hence assimilationist where possible; in some instances, accommodationist. They have also been so within their own religion. I have heard it said that the Conservative wing of Judaism broke away from the Orthodox chiefly over the questions of prohibiting driving on the Sabbath and the elimination of separate seating for women in synagogues. As for Reform Judaism, the latest joke among non-Reform Jews is that it is merely the Democratic Party platform, with holidays added.

The holiday of Hanukkah is an example of Jewish accommodation within the religion itself. For it is fairly evident, and agreed upon by Jewish scholars, that Hanukkah is not in any possible reading a major Jewish holiday. The event it marks, the Maccabean Revolt against the Seleucid Empire in the second century BC, is postbiblical, for one thing, and for another, it is built on a rather slender and unimpressive miracle: ritual oil enough to last only one day lasted for eight, hence the lighting of eight menorah candles. The persuasive explanation about Hanukkah in America is that it was elevated only because it occurred in the winter and could be used by mid-nineteenth-century Jews who wished to have a holiday that could, if not compete with, at least stand in for, Christmas. In more recent years, Jews (or some among them) have added a strong consumer touch to the holiday by presenting children with a gift on each of the eight nights that commemorative Hanukkah candles are lit.

Much has followed in the minor sociology of American Jewish life from the emphasis on Hanukkah as a Christmas surrogate. Jews send out and receive from Christian friends cards carefully denoting "Season's Greetings." Some assimilated Jewish families, who still wished to think themselves Jewish, bought and set up in their homes Christmas trees, imprecisely designated as Hanukkah bushes. Many Jewish firms and private persons give and attend Christmas parties. There are, of course, Christmas bonuses. All this is Christmas, with Jesus Christ, or its true cause, utterly subtracted.

As a secular holiday, Christmas has long been under attack. The main line of attack is the accusation that it has come to stand for little more than empty consumerism. So-called Black Friday shopping, whether it be at Target or Walmart or anywhere else, can turn ugly. Ravening crowds—screaming, pushing, and in some instances punching one another to get a bargain on Nintendo games or a toy drone at Best Buy—is not, let us agree, America at its best. Yet for a great many people it is more and more what Christmas has become. Bah, need one bother to add, humbug.

The grand shopping spree that Christmas has increasingly become has lengthened the holiday itself out to roughly a month. Shopping begins in all-too-earnest right after, if not dab on, Thanksgiving. Shops, supermarkets, and elevators are suddenly filled with canned Christmas music. One of the nice things about shopping online is that at least when doing so, one doesn't have to listen to "Rudolph the Red-Nosed Reindeer." Round late November I've found that I begin signing off emails and letters to friends with "Christmas will soon be at our throats."

I have for the most part steered clear of Christmas giving. I pass out a fifty-dollar bill to our UPS man, buy a Christmas lunch for my barber, give the attractive couple who clean our apartment every two weeks two days extra pay, write out a check for five hundred dollars for a woman who can use help providing Christmas for her own father-deserted children. My wife and I have long ceased to give each other gifts. Samuel Johnson says that man, foolish fellow, goes in life not from enjoyment to enjoyment but from want to want. Truth is, I am just about out of wants of a palpable kind: I long for no Bentleys, capacious boats, wristwatches that will tell me how many more days I have to live, exotic travel, exorbitant wines, cashmere, leather goods, lotions, or spices off the London East India boat. I am not wise, please understand—merely finished in the line of luxurious acquisition, content and grateful with what I have.

For what percentage of the 300 million or so Americans does Christmas retain its true religious meaning and, with that meaning, its power? A subtler statistician than any I have encountered may know. For those of us who find no religious significance in the holiday, it can carry complicated meanings. Everyone, surely, has heard that suicide rates go up around Christmas, occasioned by those for whom the holiday reminds them of family lost, unwanted detachments, dead-ended relationships, their own crucial missteps in life.

For the last four or five years my wife and I have by design eaten our Christmas dinner at home alone. Before this we used to dine with my wife's dear cousin Patsy and her family—a husband and three daughters and their husbands and children—in the western Chicago suburb of Oak Brook. On the Eisenhower Expressway, on the way out of the city, as we pass the Mannheim Road exit, now well into the *Judenrein* Chicago western suburbs, my long-suffering wife has had to put up with my annual Yuletide joke: "Did you note that sign, dear? Next Jew, eighty miles."

The dinner at cousin Patsy's was always excellent and the bonhomie, or in this case holiday cheer, at a perhaps too uniformly high level. Fourteen or fifteen people from the same family, and they all seemed genuinely to like one another. No bad feelings, old grudges, resentments, envy, jealousy, or hidden malice is ever allowed to leach into the turkey dressing. Over the years I've studied this extended family carefully but can find no chink in the façade of their good feeling for one another. Turns out the façade is no façade; there has never been anything other than a solid structure of family love.

Let us play the old game, "What's Wrong with This Picture?" Sixteen or seventeen people, three generations, around a table piled with holiday food. Mistletoe hangs from a nearby window. A Christmas tree, gifts beneath it, in the next room. Nordic, also Irish, good looks abound; no paucity of blond hair. Everybody seems to be enjoying him- or herself. Everyone is laughing. Except a man seated there, downtable a good bit, toward one of its corners. He is merely smiling, and it is a strange smile, less than wholehearted, with a certain tinge of irony to it. Not a very Christmassy smile, most would agree. He is, of course, *me*, the odd man out, put out there by himself.

As I was to discover some years ago, I rather like being the odd man out. I noticed this, not for the first time, in 1993, in Jerusalem, listening to Shlomo Mintz conduct the Israel Philharmonic Orchestra. Gazing around the hall, I had the following thought: *Everyone in this room may well be Jewish, and it makes me ever so slightly uncomfortable to think so.* I do not wish, apparently ever, to be among the majority; I enjoy a permanent minority status, and, I'm pleased to report, I feel it with greatest intensity as a Jew at Christmas.

Season's greetings.

CHAPTER 15

The Greatest of These Is Hope
The Impossible Promises of Christmas

Michael Graham

> And now these three remain: faith, hope, and love.
> But the one that will really stab you in the back is
> hope, that sneaky SOB.
>
> —*St. Paul, before his editors cleaned it up*

YOU CHRISTMAS SUCKERS, when are you ever going to learn?

It's all a racket, and you know it. I don't mean Santa Claus—I'm a firm believer in America's favorite noncooking fat guy. And I don't mean peace on Earth and goodwill to men and whatnot, because that's all a cover for the real Christmas scam: Hope.

To me, Christmas *is* hope, pure and simple. Love, faith, generosity—you can get that stuff from a romantic comedy on cable any night of the year. It's hope that belongs uniquely to Christmas. You can see it beaming from the kids' faces as they gaze up at the tree or squeal and squirm on a mall Santa's lap. It's why your children spend the days before Christmas poking around the presents under the tree. You look down and can tell Aunt Edna's annual "socks and underwear" lump right away. But that same package, crunched by the hands of a hopeful five-year-old, could be a lightsaber, or a robot, or a real-life dinosaur. It could be . . . anything.

And that's the problem with hope. Everything "could be."

With hope, the sky's the limit. We don't just have hopes, we have high hopes, high apple-pie-in-the-sky hopes. And so from the first time we start pumping our kids full of *The Polar Express* and *Miracle on 34th Street* the message is always that you can have anything your heart can hope for—anything at all!—if you just believe.

Which is a Christmas crock.

Let me tell you another story about presents and hope. It's called "Pandora's Box."

You probably remember the outlines of the story: Zeus discovers that Prometheus has given the gift of fire to mankind. Zeus is angry—probably because he knew how my cousin Joey and I would put this miracle to use on a future Christmas (it involved bottle rockets, tin cans, and a cat). So Zeus' revenge is to give mankind a "gift" of his own: Pandora, the first woman. And along with a stack of romance novels, a craving for chocolate, and several hundred pairs of shoes, Zeus sends Pandora to us with a beautiful box (technically it was a jar) that comes with strict instructions that it must never, ever be opened.

Of course Pandora ignores these instructions and opens the box and out fly all the evils that will plague man forever: disease, hunger, pain, and want. But at the last second Zeus prompts Pandora's hand to close the lid *just* in time to trap one final evil inside. Do you remember what it was?

Hope.

Schoolchildren are taught that the moral of Pandora's box is "hope conquers all." But the German philosopher and Hallmark Card creator Freddie Nietzsche had a different, more convincing, explanation: "Zeus gave us hope—in reality, the worst of all evils—because it prolongs the torments of Man."

Ho ho ho!

Before you dismiss me as a curmudgeon and a crank, you should know that I enjoy Christmas as much as the next guy. More, actually, because I have grasped the true miracle of the season: The fact that we aren't all dead.

Every person with a junior-high grasp of biology understands that we are living on a spinning space ball of death. Everything on this planet wants to kill us, from the water we drink (cholera) to the food we eat (salmonella) to the air we breathe (tuberculosis). The seas are filled with sharks, the land is alive with anthrax, and you know that bright star twinkling up in the heavens above? Well, one day it's going to be a Texas-sized hunk of rock and ice hurtling through space at thirty-five thousand miles an hour to scrape us off the earth. Don't believe me? Ask the dinosaurs.

Ooops. Too late.

Even Christmas itself is a death trap. Did you know people are more likely to die during the Christmas holidays than any other time? According to a study in the journal *Social Sciences and Medicine,* more people die in emergency rooms (or show up at the hospital DOA) on Christmas and New Year's Day than on any other days of the year. Heck, eleven thousand people wind up in the emergency room every year just from incidents of holiday decorating gone awry. In fact, the Product Safety Commission reports that eleven Americans manage to die every year while decking the halls. Mistletoe? Poisonous. Holly berries, ditto. Even your poinsettia can kill your cat.

So once you give up unrealistic hopes of finding a winning lottery ticket in your stocking and a blushing Kate Upton under your tree—once you internalize the astonishing unlikelihood of our survival—every day, and every Christmas, becomes a gift. Forget "glass-half-empty versus half-full." I'm just thrilled to have a glass.

To paraphrase Dante, "Abandon hope—and let's party down!"

This is the point where you, dear reader, offer me your pity. "That poor guy. He must've really had some lousy Christmases as a kid." You couldn't be more wrong. Far from a Dickensian childhood shoveling coal into Christmas stockings for Uncle Scrooge at five shillings a week, Graham family Christmases rocked.

Say what you want about the conservative, churchgoing Grahams of Lexington County, South Carolina, but we knew how to cut loose for Christmas. Growing up in the Deep South, I never had the pleasure of a white one, of course. But what we southerners lack in snowfall, we make up for in lard. And sugar. And gravy. Usually in the same dish.

My father is a lifelong fiscal conservative (aka "cheapskate"), yet Christmas was the one time of year he would crack open his wallet. Though he bragged about being "tighter than Dick's hat band"—a vaguely disquieting southernism that has something to do with frugality—my sister and I awoke to a mountain of presents every Christmas morning.

And I do mean *morning*. As evangelical Christians, we celebrated Christ's birth in the early hours of daylight, as the Good Lord intended. People who celebrate Christmas on the eve are either utterly unfamiliar with biblical teaching or Catholic. (I kid, my papist friends.)

For us, Christmas morning always exceeded expectations. The breakfast of spicy Bisquick sausage balls and "mimosas" made with sparkling grape juice never disappointed. Even the music was from Christmas Central Casting. For reasons still unclear to me, gas stations used to give away Christmas albums produced by Firestone and Goodyear (nothing says Christmas like a lube, oil, and a filter). These were all-star collections of Andy, Bing, Burl, and the gang. Mom would stack them on the record player and—assuming the arm of the record changer didn't get stuck—we'd have a nonstop soundtrack for Christmas morning.

Do I even need to say that we had a real tree? Of course we did. And not some scruffy pine from the woods behind our house, either. ("Too redneck!"—my mom.) No, sir, Dad would splurge on a Fraser fir bought from the Rotary Club. Did he do it because it sent my sister and me into paroxysms of Christmas glee? Or because it gave him an excuse to screw around with digit-endangering power tools late into the night? Only Santa knows.

I do know that the tree filled our small, seventies-prefab home with an opulent scent of celebration. When I was young, I thought every fancy cocktail party I saw in the movies must smell the way my house did on Christmas. My mom would add to the overall effect with potpourri and stacks of presents around the tree. Her philosophy on Christmas present distribution might be called the "Chicago voting" model: early and often. Just days after the tree went up, we already had significant giftage growing. By Christmas Eve it looked like a dump truck from Macy's had crashed into our living room.

I remember one Christmas morning in particular. I was nine years old, and we were having a banner day. My sister and I were exhausted from the sheer volume of presents. Shards of wrapping paper were scattered like shrapnel on the North African desert after Rommel had rolled through. We were just transitioning from the "heartfelt gratitude" portion of the program to the "Hey, that's *mine*" ceremonial combat when my dad asked, "Are you sure that's it?"

I looked under the tree. Nothing. I scanned the post-Christmas carnage. Not an unwrapped package in sight. I glanced at my mom, who was also looking around the room with a "Did I forget something in the attic?" look on her face.

(The fact that I never heard my parents rummaging around the crawlspace over my room late on Christmas Eve is proof that Santa is real.)

Then Dad nodded his head toward the upright piano along the wall. "Look over there," he said.

I waded through the wrapping paper, peered behind the piano and saw . . . something. A long, leather case leaning against the wall. I dragged it over to our floral-print sofa and laid it on the cheap, olive-green carpet at my father's feet. "Open it up," my dad said, a twinkle in his notoriously nontwinkling eyes. There was a zipper at one end. I slid it down, reached in, and pulled out something long and heavy.

"Oh, Simon!" my mother cried.

No, it wasn't a Red Ryder BB gun. (This was years before *A Christmas Story*.) It was a single-barrel, break action, 20-gauge shotgun. *A real live gun.*

There aren't actually words for what I felt in that moment. I was astonished, flabbergasted, stupefied, and more. Of course I hadn't asked Santa for a shotgun. I hadn't asked him for a Lamborghini or a date with Princess Leia either, because certain things are simply beyond a boy's imagination. My shotgun wasn't a crazy, extravagant Christmas present. It was an impossible one. And yet here I was, holding it in my hand, as my father beamed with satisfaction.

And that's when it got me. The thrill of hope.

I have very few other specific memories of my childhood Christmases after that. What I do remember are vague feelings of disappointment. It's not that my Christmases were less bright. They were the high point of my year. But when a child is convinced that Christmas is the season when impossible hopes come true, then he can only be disappointed. For no matter how glorious the gifts beneath the tree are, he has the human capacity to hope for even more.

Christmas is an irrational celebration of the limitlessness of our hopes. And yet, that's why the disappointment we inevitably feel isn't a bug. It's a feature. Unrealized hope is always there to tempt us away from the joy of what we have, the good things already grasped in our hands. Which is why every child has, at least once in his life, cried on Christmas morning.

Now that I'm a father, I'm doing my best to keep my childhood traditions alive: A real tree, spicy sausage balls, and children bursting out of their bedrooms on Christmas morning like joyous, uncaged beasts.

But my favorite moment comes the night before, in the waning hours of Christmas Eve. The children are asleep. The fading fire still burns, though darkly. Music drifts softly through the house (the same Goodyear Christmas soundtrack), and the tree stands in the red-tinged darkness, warm with lights.

I've got a drink in one hand, and the other draped over the shoulder of my wife, lying drowsily on the sofa next to me. The warm, heavy scent of the tree fills my lungs and unleashes my memories—memories of my children on Christmases past, along with fresh smiles over how giddy they'll be in the morning when they see all the wishes Santa made true.

I have hopes for my children, these four precious gifts I have been given by grace, though these hopes may seem modest to you. Other parents may fantasize about a family of Nobel Prize winners who star in Oscar-nominated movies in their spare time. Me? I just want them to be healthy, to be happy, and to avoid a few of the painful mistakes I've made. A future without sorrow or want. Is that too much for a father to hope for?

I think of my wife, nestled beside me so warm and vulnerable. Dare I hope she loves me even half as much as I love her? She doesn't talk about it often, but my wife has multiple sclerosis. Every day she wages a solitary battle against her own body, and she does it without complaint. And if that's not bad enough, she has to live with me—a husband who works in radio and writes on the side, an enthusiastic, but often inept, partner. How does she do it? Why must she? Can't she just live, without another day of worrying about bills, or struggling with her health, or being let down by her oaf of a husband?

Those days are coming, I know they are. But as I sit beside the tree, so still, so quiet in the light of the fading fire, that knowledge fades, too. I'm drawn away by my own impossible Christmas gift. By the elemental power of a simple story, whose symbols are all around me: A star. A manger. A baby, born so helpless, so alone. And yet somehow, so full of hope.

I don't notice it, but my eyes are moist. My throat is dry. And there in the pale light of the glistening tree, hope envelops me like swaddling clothes. It warms me like the breath of a newborn child. It fills my lungs. It pumps the very blood through my heart. I close my eyes. I bow my head.

And I believe.

CHAPTER 16

Saint Joseph
The Forgotten "Father Christmas"

Christopher Buckley

HARK, ALL YE FATHERS, who in the wee hours of Christmas Eve find yourselves half in the bag from a surfeit of eggnog or Martinis—or both, thereof—grumbling and cursing as you contemplate the electric train set (116 parts) and the Victorian doll house (424 parts)—verily, still in their boxes. Why—thou fools, thou knaves—didst thou wait until this late hour to confront these most fearsome words: "Some assembly required"?

Yet tremble not. You are not alone. Someone watcheth over you. Verily.

The Catholic Church has a patron saint for pretty much every occasion and situation, from lost causes (St. Jude) to lost objects (St. Anthony), baldness (St. Bartholomew), and gum disease (St. Apollonia). Saint Joseph is not specifically invoked as the patron saint of unassembled toys on Christmas Eve, but he should be, for he does watch over us. I know. I have seen him, lo, on many a tipsy Christmas Eve, while nothing doth stir in all the house, except stupid me. On that first Christmas Eve, who got the manger ready in that ratty stable in Bethlehem? And decent Joe that he was, he probably wasn't snockered on Scotch and barking at Mary because he couldn't find his bleeping hammer.

Certainly St. Joseph could be forgiven if he *had* been grumpy that night. Consider—earlier that year, his wife had handed him a bit of a surprise, informing him that she was pregnant. By, uh, the Holy Spirit.

Most guys would not greet with unbridled joy the news that they'd been superseeded by a "spirit," never mind how "holy." The *let-me-get-this-straight* possibilities are endless. But St. Joseph neither blew his top nor lost his cool, to use two phrases probably not current in AD 1.

As the Gospel of St. Matthew informs us, "Joseph, being a just man and unwilling to put her to shame, resolved to divorce her quietly." The operative word there is "quietly." For "put her to shame" meant: Allow her to be stoned to death for adultery. Jewish law in those days was pretty stern stuff.

Though Matthew doesn't mention it, St. Joseph at this point may have been kicking himself for not having insisted on a prenup. At any rate, what a dilemma the poor guy was handed. *Thank you, Holy Spirit.* As for "quietly" divorcing—tricky. Recent scholarship has shown that back then, El Al had no direct flights to Reno, Haiti, or Tijuana.

Joseph now had a dream in which he was visited by an angel. In English lit this is called the *deus ex machina,* Latin for, "In case of Third Act problems, resort to this."

It was the first of four such dreams. Joseph ought to be in the *Guinness Book of Records* for "New Testament Figure Most Visited by an Angel While Dreaming." By the fourth visitation, he was surely muttering, "Oy gevalt, *again?*"

In Matthew's telling, the angel's message was both straightforward and ambiguous: "Joseph, son of David, do not fear to take Mary your wife, for that which is conceived of her is of the Holy Spirit." It's straightforward insofar as: *Your wife has been impregnated by the Holy Spirit.* Ambiguous because "do not fear to take Mary your wife" would appear to make little sense. Two verses earlier, Joseph is identified as "her husband." So he has already taken Mary as his wife.

I stipulate that, my Greek, Latin, and Hebrew being rusty (actually, nonexistent), I am unable to check the translation. Maybe "take" means "put up with." Wait. Is Matthew here prefiguring the coming, two thousand years hence, of Henny Youngman? "Take my wife—please!" Hmm.

A few verses later, we come to the slightly indelicate matter of Joseph and Mary's connubial arrangement. Joseph wakes up from his dream—surely muttering *WTF?* And "as the angel of the Lord commanded him; he took his wife, but knew her not until she had borne him a son."

Two observations. First, Joseph demonstrates that he is a mensch of the first order. A credulous mensch, perhaps, but a mensch all the same. Second, in order to fulfill the prophecy that the Messiah would be born of a virgin (Isaiah 7:14), Mary had to remain *intacta* until Jesus was born. Matthew tells us that following the blessed event, Joseph was permitted—finally, poor guy—to consummate their marriage.

Much as I would prefer to draw the curtain there and leave the nice young married couple in peace, the narrative presents us with a difficulty. For if Jesus was not biologically related to Joseph, then how could he be "the son of David"? (See Matthew 1:1.) He is referred to as such no fewer than *nine times* in Matthew. But it's Joseph who is related to David, not Mary.[1]

In the opening verses of his Gospel, Matthew goes to great pains to establish Jesus' direct lineal descent from David—indeed, all the way back to Abraham. Matthew's interminable

---

1. In the court of the French King Louis XVI there was a certain Duchesse de Noailles. Her nickname was "Madame L'etiquette," owing to her obsession with etiquette and court formalities. She was crazy as a bedbug. To take just one example, she carried on an extended correspondence with the Virgin Mary, Mary being ghosted by the Duchess' confessor, who was trying to humor the old girl. (What a job!) One day, the Virgin Mary committed a faux pas, socially speaking, in her correspondence. The Duchess explained it away to her household saying, "You see, she only married into the House of David."

genealogy also *inflicted* great pain, as any Catholic schoolboy or girl who had to memorize those bloody sixteen verses will attest. I still twitch whenever I hear "Abraham begat Isaac; and Isaac begat Jacob . . . and Ezekiel begat Manassas." (Fortunately, you don't hear it all that often.) From Abraham to Jesus is forty-two generations, which is a lot of begatting.

So: if Joseph didn't contribute DNA to Jesus, how could Jesus be related to David and Abraham? You and I may not stay up at night gnawing the bed linen fretting over this, but reconciling Jesus' divine and Davidic paternity caused all manner of doctrinal mayhem among the early Church fathers. They actually cared about this stuff. That was their job.

A hundred and fifty years after Jesus' birth, there appeared a text called the Protoevangelium, or Gospel of James. It purported to be a prequel—as it were—to the Nativity narratives of Matthew and Luke. (Mark doesn't mention Joseph at all; John makes only a glancing reference to the Holy Family.) At any rate, the Protoevangelium asserted that Mary *remained* a virgin after Jesus' birth, contradicting Matthew. It was a must-read document among early Christians, very popular. But it caused a lot of argument, and probably fistfights. The Church fathers finally solved the problem by declaring it apocryphal, which is the doctrinal term for "Nah."

Still arguments raged, and trying to follow them will give you a headache. Finally, twelve centuries later, Thomas Aquinas found a solution by declaring that Joseph was not some mere bystander, but was essential to the whole concept of the Incarnation. Why? Remove Joseph and unmarried, pregnant Mary goes down in a hail of stones. Viewed in this light, Joseph is the ultimate beard. Certainly he is the ultimate husband—especially if, as the Protowhatever averred, he never got any.

In Joseph's second dream, the angel warned him to take the Holy Family and flee into Egypt, because Herod, livid at being informed by the Magi that a future king had been born, was going to slaughter every Judean male child under two years old.

The third dream told Joseph it was now okay to come back to Israel. The fourth said to avoid Judea. Herod's son, no improvement on dad, was now ruler. Joseph should go to Galilee. So, after a schlepping of literally biblical proportion, Joseph finally settled the family in Nazareth, a far from fashionable venue. As Bette Davis famously described it, "What a dump."

Joseph is mentioned only once more—not in Matthew, but in Luke. Jesus is twelve now, about bar mitzvah age. At Passover time, Joseph and Mary take Him to Jerusalem, which must have seemed to be a relief after Nazareth. Jesus appears to have liked Jerusalem, because when it was time to go home, He disappeared. He didn't learn much about the virtue of "obedience" from his dad, who himself set the gold standard. But to be fair, Joseph and Mary do seem to have been a bit casual in the chaperone department. They managed to walk all the way back to Nazareth—a real schlep—before either of them said to the other, "I thought He was with *you.*"

Frantic, Joseph and Mary hoof it back to Jerusalem, look everywhere, and finally find Jesus in the Temple, where He's dazzling the rabbis with his commentary on Scripture. Joseph and Mary are in no mood to *kvell.* They tell Him they've been out of their minds with worry. Does Jesus say, "Sorry"? Oh, no. He sniffs, "How is it you sought me? Did you not know that I must be in my Father's house?"

Hello? Here His parents are sick with worry, their feet blistered, and He's giving them attitude? Thank you, Little "Lord" Fauntleroy. And how nice of Him to remind Joseph, after everything he's done for Him, that *You're not my real father.* Such was Joseph's reward for being a devoted husband and father, and without ever having uttered a word of complaint. Or any word, for that matter. Joseph doesn't have a single line of dialogue in any of the Gospels (though this does make him an ideal

Jewish husband). The scene in the Temple is our last glimpse of Joseph. We don't even hear, *And eventually Joseph died, his heart being broken.*

One could speculate. Suppose that after they got the kid back to Nazareth, Joseph said, "You know, I'm not feeling the love here." Suppose he decided, *enough* and took a sabbatical from being "Saint" Joseph, Perfect Husband, Terrific Dad. But Joseph, being Joseph, wouldn't have done that. Whatever happened to him, I hope he did find some love in the end. He sure earned it.

He did, in a way, but it took a long time—fifteen centuries. As Thomas J. Craughwell explains in *Saints Preserved: An Encyclopedia of Relics:*

> Saint Joseph was a casualty of the early Church's often violent controversies regarding the nature of Christ, whether he was truly God, or a specially selected man, or was both God and man simultaneously. The debate that raged around the issue precluded the development of devotion to Saint Joseph—it would only be asking for more. And so as love for the Blessed Virgin and her parents Anne and Saint Joachim flourished, Joseph remained a bit player who attracted very little notice. As a result, no place claimed to possess his tomb or remains.

His comeback began in the 1500s and 1600s, first courtesy of the Carmelites and then by the new order of Jesuits, who were the Navy SEALs and Delta Force of the Counter-Reformation. In 1870 Pope Pius IX made Joseph patron of the Universal Church. He asserted (*ahem*, absent scriptural authority) that

St. Joseph had died in "the arms of Jesus and Mary," making him the patron saint of a happy death. It's lovely to think that's how it ended for this splendid man. (Though it would have been nice to hear Matthew or Luke or *someone* say that's how it went down.)

Later, in 1889, Pope Leo XIII issued an encyclical urging Catholics to pray to St. Joseph. His popularity blossomed. He became a fashionable patron saint, and the list of countries claiming him as theirs is now long and diverse, from Canada to Vietnam.

He became political, too. In 1955, at the height of the Cold War, Pope Pius XII slyly designated May 1 as the Feast of St. Joseph the Worker, this being May Day, which commie dictatorships honored with clanking parades of missiles, tanks, goosestepping soldiers, and giant posters of those humanitarians, Stalin and Mao. Somewhere on the instrument panel of his B-52 bomber in the movie *Dr. Strangelove*, Slim Pickens might have had a St. Joseph medal.

And now many saints get to be a drug brand? My generation's first headaches were alleviated by St. Joseph's Bayer Aspirin for children.

For about fifteen years or so, until my children's presents no longer required "some assembly," I celebrated St. Joseph's feast day not on May 1 or March 19 (its current slot), but on December 24 and on into the early hours of December 25.

A little over a century ago, a prayer containing a series of petitions, or litany, to St. Joseph was formally approved by the then-pope. It lists all his holy attributes, including "Light of Patriarchs," "Chaste guardian of the Virgin"—which would appear to clinch the argument made by the Protoevangelium-ists —and "Foster Father of the Son of God." It continues, calling him the "Mirror of patience, Lover of poverty, Model of artisans" and enough encomia to keep even the most modest saint blushing for another two millennia.

No less than his due. Had the Vatican put me on the St. Joseph Litany Committee back in 1909, I'd have noted some of his other outstanding qualities:

> Assembler most diligent,
> Locator of Part 7b,
> Repairer of Part 45c,
> Provider of socket head screw,
> And of (@#$%-ing) hex key.
>
> Bearer of aspirin,
> Forestaller of hangover,
> Comforter and companion.
> Mensch without equal.
> Amen.

CHAPTER 17

Mary, Mother of All

The Real Miracles of the Virgin Birth Aren't What You Think

Mollie Hemingway

MY CHILDREN shower me with affection, so I have no real reason to go fishing for more love. But I do it anyway. The problem is, when I ask if they love Mommy or Daddy more, they always insist that they love us equally. Sometimes I load the question the way political pollsters do: "Daddy has been working late a lot and sometimes yells at you. Mommy is a great snuggler, makes all your favorite meals, and taught you to ride a bike recently. Who do you love more, Mommy or Daddy?"

But even then, the kids insist they love us both the same. It's touching. And also infuriating.

Even worse is what they say when I sometimes fish for a world's greatest mom trophy. (Don't judge; we all do it.) I thought there was only one answer to the question, "Who's the best mother in the world?" And that the answer is always: "You, Mom!" Oh, no. When I ask my kids, "Who's the best momma in the whole world?" They always reply, "Mary, mother of God!"

They're careful to insist that I'm absolutely, positively, a solid second. Which isn't bad, I guess. After all, Mary is—literally—the most blessed woman in the history of the world. We Christians know this because God chose her as the one woman throughout all space and time to deliver humanity its Savior. And if you needed even more proof, when God chose her—which was probably the biggest surprise any human being has ever experienced—she responded with a brief moment of confusion followed by serene, lifelong acceptance. Most of us struggle to achieve serene acceptance at the checkout line at the grocery store. So yes, she's the best mother.

And her unique role in the history of humanity is never more apparent than at Christmas.

We moderns have a variety of beliefs about Jesus' birth. Some of us confidently accept every last miracle richly detailed in the Gospels. Others pick and choose—they'll accept that God became flesh and dwelt among us for our salvation, but the star guiding the Wise Men is a bridge too far. Others reject the story in toto.

A few years ago the *New York Times'* Nick Kristof mocked the Virgin Birth in a column published on the Roman Catholic feast of Mary's assumption into heaven (just to ensure the maximum amount of implied insult). Kristof was worried because 83 percent of Americans say they believe in the Virgin Birth of Jesus. He said this belief separates us from the rest of the industrialized world—and he didn't mean it in a good way.

"The faith in the Virgin Birth reflects the way American Christianity is becoming less intellectual and more mystical over time," Kristof wrote, remarking with horror that the percentage of Americans who believe in the Virgin Birth had actually risen five points since the question was last polled. "I'm troubled by the way the great intellectual traditions of Catholic and Protestant churches alike are withering," he tsked. Though he didn't specify when, exactly, Christians had not believed in the Virgin Birth. Which was first mentioned, you know, in the Bible.

Kristof wondered why more Christians couldn't be like his Presbyterian grandfather, who rejected the notion of Mary's virginity. Which is an odd stance, since you can't really be a Christian without believing in Christianity. But not as odd as Kristof's follow-up claim: that the "evidence for the Virgin Birth" was "shaky." If you're looking for forensic proof of the deepest mysteries of God's love, then you're in the wrong business.

It's easy to understand why our modern cultural elites struggle with the science of the Virgin Birth, the heavens filling with angels, and the star of the Magi. Yet if you think about it, these miracles aren't even close to being the most difficult things to believe about the Nativity story.

The deepest mystery of Christmas isn't how Jesus was conceived and born—it's why. Why would Almighty God care so much about losers like us that He would humble Himself to take on human flesh and enter humanity at such a low station? As the sixteenth-century hymn "From Heaven above to Earth I Come" puts it,

> Welcome to earth, O noble Guest,
> Through whom the sinful world is blest!
> You came to share my misery
> That You might share Your joy with me.
>
> Ah, Lord, though You created all,
> How weak You are, so poor and small,
> That You should choose to lay Your head
> Where lowly cattle lately fed.

As intellectually and technologically advanced as we've become, this incarnation of God in the person of Christ Jesus is just as unfathomable to us as it was to Mary, Joseph, the shepherds, and the Wise Men two thousand years ago.

Saint Bernard of Clairvaux, a doctor of the Church, held that there were three miracles present in the Christmas story. The first was that God would be joined with human flesh. The second was that He would be born of a virgin. The third was that Mary would have such profound faith that she would accept God's word. Sure, she asked a few questions. But once those were answered, she believed.

So let's revisit the story. Mary, whose name means "bitter," was born to Joachim and Anna, poor parents who lived at a time of general suffering for the Jews. She's not a woman of means or of particularly high station. She's almost certainly shockingly young—probably a young teenager. We learn from Luke that the angel who is sent tells her, "Rejoice, highly favored one, the Lord is with you; blessed are you among women!" Mary seems rather taken aback by this heavenly greeting, so the angel tells her, "Do not be afraid, Mary, for you have found favor with God." He tells her she's going to conceive Jesus and that not only will He be a ruler—He will be the Son of God.

Thunderstruck, Mary wonders how she could carry a child, because she's never had sexual relations with a man. (It says a lot about Mary that this detail is presented more as pious wondering and a wish for clarification than questioning or doubt.) The angel tells her the Holy Spirit will come upon her and that "with God nothing will be impossible." Oh, well then. Okay.

At which point Mary simply says, "Let it be done to me according to your word." She declares herself to be God's servant, and submits entirely to His impossible Word. Which, if you would just stop and reflect on it for a moment, is amazing.

At the same time all this craziness is going on, Mary's cousin Elizabeth—well advanced in age, and believed to be barren—is somehow already pregnant with none other than John the Baptist. When Mary is told this, she heads over to the hill country where Elizabeth lives. As she arrives, John leaps "for joy" in Elizabeth's womb. Mary then offers her famous song, the "Magnificat" in Christian liturgy, in response:

> My soul magnifies the Lord,
> and my spirit has rejoiced in God my Savior.
> For He has regarded the lowly state of His maidservant;
> for behold, henceforth all generations will call me
>   blessed.
> For He who is mighty has done great things for me,
> and holy is His name.
> And His mercy is on those who fear Him
> from generation to generation.
> He has shown strength with His arm;
> He has scattered the proud in the imagination of their
>   hearts.
> He has put down the mighty from their thrones,
> and exalted the lowly.
> He has filled the hungry with good things,
> and the rich He has sent away empty.
> He has helped His servant Israel,
> in remembrance of His mercy,
> as He spoke to our fathers,
> to Abraham and to His seed forever.

It's a breathtaking exultation that tells us a great deal about the nature of God. He delights in lifting up the poor and humble, while bringing down the rich and mighty, for instance. But Mary's words tell us just as much about God's chosen vessel. She is carrying the living God in her womb but she doesn't act holier-than-thou or proud. Her humility is so pure that she isn't even conscious of it. Humility isn't second nature to Mary; it's her first nature.

Such humility, such trust, runs directly counter to the nature of the rest of us—even Joseph. Because after all of this, Mary still has to explain to her betrothed that, oops, she's pregnant. According to the letter of the law, Joseph could have had her killed. Instead he resolves to privately dissolve the engagement so as to preserve her reputation. This might sound like mercy, but imagine how small a mercy it must have felt to Mary: She had done nothing wrong but had to carry on courageously in the face of her betrothed cutting her loose.

Fortunately for our heroine, Gabriel then visits Joseph in a dream, and he also chooses to believe. Yet even in the midst of this cosmic drama, there are quotidian things going on in the world: Like, for instance, Caesar demanding a census. So Mary and Joseph adhere to the law of the land by traveling to Bethlehem to be recorded. Presumably they had no idea the housing situation would be so bad once they got there. Maybe they thought they could stay with family. Maybe they thought there would be rooms at the inn. Maybe they believed they were blessed to have any shelter at all.

In retrospect, if the people of Bethlehem had any clue what was happening in their midst, they would have rushed to help Mary. Instead of laboring in a stable, Mary would have given birth in comfort. Instead of being wrapped in swaddling clothes and laid in a manger, Jesus would have been robed in the finest fabric. But the truth is also that whether the people of Bethlehem knew the incarnate God was being born that night or not, they should have helped this poor couple. (And if we think we would have been better, this is a pretty good time to ask ourselves if we're doing right by young families in our own neighborhoods.)

Art from the Middle Ages shows Mary joining Joseph in adoration of the Christ child immediately after His birth. It makes for a pretty picture, of course, but it airbrushes the real trials of childbirth and postpartum delivery. Jesus may be true God but He's also true man. That means He was a true baby, who did all the things true babies do—crying, eating, peeing, crying some more. And Mary may have been highly favored, but she was still a true woman—one who had just pushed out a child on a dirt floor after riding for days on the back of a donkey. Again, the example of Mary is a fine thing to remember the next time you have to wipe a runny nose or deal with a particularly viscous diaper explosion. The lowliest work of motherhood is still a holy blessing, and Mary was offered no reprieve from these duties. Mary may be the most blessed among all women, but she was a true woman herself. She had to figure out how to be a mother with no one there to guide her. Mary's Christmas virtue is all the more amazing because she was a real woman going through real troubles—just like the rest of us.

And that's why, in the "who's your favorite (non-Jesus) person in the Bible or church history" parlor game, Mary is a fan favorite. (She's way ahead of every other figure, as evidenced by all the art and hymnody surrounding her story—not to mention all the children named Mary, Miriam, Marilyn, and—ahem—Mollie.) In the midst of a hectic life in a hectic world, her incredible, incorruptible faith can make her seem nearly impossible to relate to. But she was meant not just for Jesus—she was meant for all of us.

Jesus Himself holds her up as a model for all Christians. At one point in the Gospel of Luke, a woman listening to Jesus in a crowd cries out to Him, "Blessed is the womb that bore You, and the breasts which nursed You!" He says, "More than that, blessed are those who hear the word of God and keep it!"

On first reading, this might sound like a slight. But it's not. Jesus isn't saying, "Sure, but . . ." He's saying "Yes, and . . ." That the Virgin Mary bore Jesus and nursed Him and raised Him is beautiful and holy. And yet it pales in comparison to Mary's joyful confession that she is the Lord's handmaiden and that she will follow His Word wherever it leads.

She is blessed simply because she was chosen to be the mother of God—but she is a blessing because of the way she made that choice. She said yes, not just to Gabriel's unprecedented invitation, but to everything God asked of her. She assented completely, giving over not just her body—which, let's face it, is asking a lot—but also her heart.

Somehow, it's not hard to imagine a *New York Times* columnist echoing the complaint that Christianity—and especially Catholic Christianity—is inherently sexist, what with having little, if any, place for women. As in her day, Mary's story is met with suspicion, even scorn. Yet it was a lowly woman that God entrusted with the most important role of all—carrying Himself for forty long weeks and pushing Him into the world. "For unto us a Child is born" would not have been possible without Mary's womanhood.

Many of my fellow Protestants are a bit weirded out by Marian devotion among Roman Catholics—the May crowning, the statues, the Rosary. And certainly some traditions have made Mary into an object of worship, a co-redeemer, and one to whom prayers are offered. But just because some go too far doesn't mean any of us should ignore Mary. We remember and honor her so that we may remember how God chose to be with us; we remember and honor her by seeking to make her words our own: "I am the Lord's servant/maidservant! I have heard Your Word, O Lord, and can only say, Amen!"

Through Mary, God gave Jesus to all mankind. And Jesus gave her back to all mankind as He hung on the cross, telling John—and all of us—"Behold your mother!" Mary isn't God. She's not above God, she's not equal to God. But given her starring role in the Nativity story, we can all agree that she is even more than just the mother of God. She is the model for, and mother of, all Christians.

Martin Luther, the reformer and pastor of St. Mary's Church in Wittenberg, gave a Christmas sermon in 1529 where he said of Mary that she "is the Mother of Jesus and the Mother of all of us even though it was Christ alone who reposed on her knees. . . . If He is ours, we ought to be in His situation; there where He is, we ought also to be and all that He has ought to be ours, and His mother is also our mother."

My children agree. And they're right. Mary is mother to us all—and she's the best mother in the whole world.

CHAPTER 18

The First Noel

Christmas with Jesus

Kirsten Powers

IN MY UNORTHODOX childhood, Christmas was as an oasis of normalcy. It was the one day of the year I could count on some sort of harmony in my divided family.

At age five, my parents divorced and established two outposts in my life, from which I shuttled back and forth. One home was headed by my sophisticated, East Coast-born, feminist mother; the other by my down-to-earth, Idaho-bred father, who held fast to his traditionalist views. After they split, my younger brother, Matt, and I lived with my mother during the week and decamped to my father's house for the weekends.

When I was ten, I moved in with my father, who by then had remarried. From that point on I spent weekends and summers with my mother. Through the shifting home lives I absorbed just enough of each of my parent's personalities and worldviews to make me feel like an interloper wherever I was. Except on Christmas.

The Christmas season was a magical time, made all the more special because I got to experience the magic twice. I helped pick out and decorate two Christmas trees, one at my mother's house and one at my father's. Wherever we woke up on Christmas morning, my brother and I were greeted by mountains of presents piled under the tree. We would spend hours plowing through them and then look at each other with delight as we realized we would get to do it all over again just a few hours later at the other house. Christmas meant two of everything.

Or rather, almost everything: Church we only did once. My mother was a lapsed Catholic who had no discernable faith; my father was an Episcopalian who took us to church every Sunday. Going to the Christmas Eve service with him was a high point of the holiday season. We lit candles and sang carols, and all felt right with the world. I suppose we talked some about Jesus, but truth be told, my mind was primarily occupied with counting down the hours until the commencement of presents.

Looking back now, I see that Christmas in my family—like it is in lots of families—was really a cultural event focused on the exchange of gifts. It had next to nothing to do with the birth of Christ Jesus.

I continued to cherish Christmas well into my adulthood, probably because it conjured up so many happy childhood memories. I never dwelt on the religious aspect. In fact, during my sophomore year of college I fell into an existential crisis of faith. As I teetered on the edge of disbelief, I called my father looking for reassurance. Instead, he confided to me that as much as he had struggled to believe—and at times had possessed a genuine, but fragile faith—he had come to the unhappy conclusion that God wasn't real. He and my mother were both archaeologists, and my father's religious belief had been somewhat controversial in his professional life, where his colleagues viewed themselves as scientists who were supposed to be above such primitive superstitions. He explained that even though he had wrestled with his faith throughout my childhood, he had continued to take us to church because he believed it was good for my brother and me to be exposed to the values of Christianity.

As he explained his disbelief to me, I was deeply unsettled—feeling as though I was tumbing through space, grasping for something, anything, to break my fall. The sensation was physical. I was suddenly untethered, and I felt as though I could barely breathe. I hadn't wanted him to confirm my doubts. But there it was: If my father—the most brilliant man I knew—didn't believe in Christianity, then it couldn't be true. And so I fell away, too.

At first, my disbelief was fairly benign, but as I grew older it morphed into something more contemptuous. By the time I was in my thirties I found the idea of religion, and particularly Christianity, utterly preposterous. I had moved from Washington to New York, and my professional and social lives were rooted in Democratic politics. I didn't know anyone who wasn't liberal, and the majority of my friends and colleagues were atheists.

I didn't know any serious Christians either, but nonetheless I was sure they were all anti-intellectual rubes and probably misogynists to boot. In hindsight, I realize that I had no paradigm through which to understand devout religious belief, because I had never been exposed to it. Even the people I had known who called themselves Christians didn't seem to take the teachings of the Bible all that seriously; they would pick and choose as it suited them. I couldn't understand why anyone would insist they had to follow all the teachings of the Bible. How unenlightened! And the concept of submitting to a higher authority wasn't especially attractive either. I liked doing what I wanted and not being accountable to anyone.

During this time I was single, and friends set me up on a lot of dates. When they asked me if there were any deal breakers, I explained there was only one: No religious people.

Shortly after I made that declaration, I started dating a guy who mentioned, in passing, that he attended a Presbyterian church. I flinched. But I liked him, and because I was so religiously illiterate, I didn't understand that some Presbyterian churches are evangelical. I assumed he was a cultural Christian, like the few other Christians I knew. After all, I told myself, he was too smart to actually believe the Bible. So we continued to date.

A few months into the relationship he confronted me with a question I didn't expect to get from any person I knew: "Do you accept Jesus Christ as your Savior?"

"Of course not!" I answered. It was ridiculous. *Who says things like this?* I wondered. The entire exchange was alarming. *Was he some kind of religious zealot?* I asked myself. *What's happening?*

My boyfriend then explained that he saw a future for us, but that he couldn't marry someone who didn't accept Jesus as their Savior. I was sad, because this meant he was soon to be my ex-boyfriend. But then he told me something that I had never heard: "If you can keep an open mind," he said, "God can reveal Himself to you."

This didn't sound right to me, but I had so much respect for this man that I didn't feel I could dismiss his claim out of hand. I remember thinking to myself, *What if he's right—and I don't even try?*

So I agreed to start going to church with him, occasionally. But I warned him that even though I was willing to show up at church from time to time, the chances of me becoming a Christian were less than zero.

Everything about the evangelical culture of his church repelled me: They met in an auditorium and there was a band, drums, and the whole contemporary Christian shebang. I had been used to the high-church liturgy of the Episcopalians with incense and sacred music. I stood in horror as I listened to congregants at my boyfriend's church belt out cheesy love songs to Jesus. But it turned out that the church he attended was pastored by a man named Tim Keller, who might be the most persuasive Christian apologist and evangelical pastor of his generation (if not the century).

When Keller spoke, I was mesmerized. I learned later that Keller's ministry is a "seeker church" for the unchurched in Manhattan, which meant that his sermons were always based on the assumption that he needed to persuade the many skeptics in the audience. Each week he would make the case for Christianity and against our secular age. His sermons would weave together threads from philosophy, history, music, literature, and even popular culture. Through them, he demonstrated how the Gospel applied to our lives and deftly examined and rebutted challenges to the Christian story. I had never heard anyone talk about the Bible, or Jesus, the way Keller did. And so he began chipping away at my unbelief.

I told my boyfriend it was okay for him to pray for us. Then I started to pray, too. I asked God to reveal Himself to me. I took up reading the Bible. In a seemingly nonchalant moment— which I now know was anything but—my boyfriend gave me Sheldon Vanauken's *A Severe Mercy*, which is the story of a married couple's journey from atheism to belief. Vanauken had been a professor at Oxford, and the book recounts the time he spent hashing out the Bible's claims with his fellow professors, who were themselves strong believers. It was the first I had heard of intellectuals adhering to an orthodox belief in Jesus. (And yes, I realize now how stupid that sounds.)

About a year into this unlikely journey I came to the conclusion that the weight of evidence was on the side of Christianity being true. But this was a head decision, not one of the heart.

Shortly after arriving at that conclusion, I went on a business trip to Taiwan. During the travel I prayed fervently that God would reveal Himself to me, though I didn't really understand what I was asking for. And then one morning I awoke from a dream in which Jesus had come to me and said, "Here I am." I was overwhelmed and frightened because the experience was so real.

I called my boyfriend, half a world away, but before I had a chance to tell him, he broke up with me. I can see now that his purpose in my life had been fulfilled, but at the time it was quite a shock, if for no other reason than the fact that he was the only Christian I really knew well. Who was I going to talk to about this dream?

I ended up reaching out to a Christian I had met through my (now ex-) boyfriend and uncomfortably recounted my dream to him. He himself had become a believer through a dream and insisted that I needed to join a Bible study. The idea scared me, since (1) I had never been to a Bible study, and (2) I associated such things with religious fanaticism.

But I was desperate. Ever since the dream, I had felt the constant presence of God. I actually thought I might be going crazy. In fact, I was so worried that I began dodging my Jewish therapist, who, as far as I knew, was nonreligious. When she tracked me down one day on the phone I explained I didn't want to tell her what was going on because she might have me committed. After much prodding, I told her the story. I'll never forget her response: "You are not going crazy, Kirsten. Now you just know there is another dimension to life."

So I took a breath and headed to the Upper East Side Bible study my friend had suggested. I wish I could remember exactly what was said that first day, because as I stepped out onto the sidewalk after the meeting I was overwhelmed by the truth of the Gospels. It was—as they say—as though the scales had fallen from my eyes. Suddenly everything looked different. I marveled to myself, "It's true. It's completely true."

I was briefly overwhelmed by joy, but it didn't last. The next

186 • THE FIRST NOEL

few years were a roller coaster of belief and disbelief as I struggled to transition from my worldly life to one rooted in God.

But eventually God won out. He always does.

Ironically, after all of this, Christmas lost its luster for me. The
rank materialism became too much to bear, and the Christmas
season morphed from being a time I savored into something
I tried to survive each year. Santa Claus, Christmas trees, the
holiday jingles—they all felt like pagan oppression. As the great
Christian pastor A. W. Tozer wrote, "In our mad materialism
we have turned beauty into ashes, prostituted every normal
emotion and made merchandise of the holiest gift the world
ever knew. . . . Not peace but tension, fatigue and irritation
rule the Christmas season." When people complained about
a war on Christmas I often smirked and thought to myself,
Where do I sign up? Honestly: When a sale at Crate & Barrel gets
entangled with the birth of Jesus Christ, something has gone
horribly wrong.

I had come a long way from my disbelieving days when I was
a happy participant in the festival of Christmas consumerism.
When I was in my twenties, a friend who had grown up in a
Christian family told me that when he was a child, he and his
siblings didn't get Christmas presents. Instead, they were given
money to purchase presents for children who had less. At the
time, I had thought this tradition bordered on child abuse.
Now it sounded perfectly sensible.

It wasn't Christmas, but Easter that became the home for
my heart. The evening Easter Vigil I attended at my Anglican
church was magical in ways my childhood self could never
have understood as she delighted in her Christmas traditions.
Shrouded in darkness for the first two-thirds of the three-hour
service, we would be overwhelmed by the gloom of Jesus' cru-

cifixion and death. Then, there was an explosion of light, song, and joy as the priest proclaimed the Resurrection.

The birth of Jesus was important, I told myself. But how could it compare with the Resurrection? What could be more glorious than a victorious Savior rising from the dead?

But then I realized that I had allowed the secular celebrations of Christmas to crowd out its transcendent meaning. There could be no Resurrection without the Incarnation. As theologian N. T. Wright points out, it's Christmas that is the moment when God launched a "divine rescue mission" of humankind. It's when, as Scripture tells us, "the Word became flesh and made His dwelling among us."

God didn't just condescend to come to earth as a human. He came as a helpless infant. The King of Kings was born amid barnyard animals and piles of hay after His lowly parents were turned away from better lodgings. When the Magi came to see the Lord, there was no security on hand to judge whether they were worthy. The Messiah was approachable. He was both one of us, and at the same time, "God with us." He was flesh. He would hunger, He would bleed, He would love, He would thirst, and He would die.

One of the unfathomable mysteries of Christmas is that the infant Jesus was born a sacrifice. His story had already been written: After a short ministry, Jesus would be unjustly accused, betrayed, humiliated, tortured, abandoned, and crucified. All for our sake. As Isaiah foretold, "He was pierced for our transgressions, He was crushed for our iniquities; the punishment that brought us peace was on Him, and by His wounds we are healed." None of this could have happened had He not been born fully human.

There's even more beauty than that, if you can believe it. At every turn in the story of Christmas we witness unquestioning obedience to God. A young virgin is told she will conceive a son by the Holy Spirit. How will she explain this to her husband-to-be? What if he refuses to marry her and she's left to bear a son out of wedlock? These were not minor concerns in the time in which she lived. Still, her response to the angel Gabriel is profound in its simplicity. "I am the Lord's servant," Mary says. "May your word to me be fulfilled." How many of us are slower to respond to God's prompting over much smaller matters?

Joseph was just as quick to ignore his worldly concerns and acquiesce to the call of God. Upon learning the news of Mary's pregnancy, he decided to quietly end the engagement so as to not expose her to public disgrace. But mercifully, he, too, had a dream. An angel of the Lord appeared to him and told him to "not be afraid" to take Mary as his wife. When Joseph awoke, "He did what the angel commanded." He didn't ask his friends to weigh in on the situation. He didn't start a prayer chain to discern what God was calling him to do. He obeyed. And then he and Mary joined in their obedience to welcome into the world the Light of all mankind.

Christmas is a day to remember all of this; to ponder the mystery and the wonder of a birth like no other.

What a gift! It's one I won't take for granted again.

CHAPTER 19

The Day After

The Illusion of Returning to Normal

James Lileks

THE DAY AFTER Christmas is called Boxing Day because you are legally permitted to punch anyone who plays that Alvin and the Chipmunks song.

That's one of the joys that awaits when your eyes crack open on December 26: No more Christmas music. No more over-emoted bathetic bombast blared out by a pop singer in a California studio in June. No more "Rockin' around the Christmas Tree," which is impossible if your tree is in the corner, as ours usually is. At best we can rock *around* it in a semicircular fashion. No more "Rudolph the Red-Nosed Reindeer," with its expectation that we're heartened by the other reindeer's craven change of heart once the bossman singles out the mutant. *Oh I always said you should be involved in the reindeer games, Rudolph.* Yeah, stuff it, Vixen.

The day after is a grand day. No more worries. No more doubts about whether you got your spouse the right thing. You didn't, but everyone performed their roles well; she was appreciative, and loved it, and it was just *darling*, and by mutual unspoken agreement she knows the sales slip is under the tissue paper. Your toddler daughter was ecstatic when she unwrapped the box of Pink-Hued Petrochemicals Pressed Mechanically Extruded into the Shape of a Castle for a Medieval City-State Apparently Run by Small Ponies. You assembled it at 7:00 a.m.

on Christmas morning, wondering about the mood of the Shanghai serf who tied the twisty plastic so tightly to the cardboard packaging that it took bolt cutters to free the pieces. So that's done. Your dog liked the Elk Femur you gave him and is probably outside in the snow working on it, feeling all wolfish and authentic. It was a wonderful Christmas, and here's another reason to beam:

No beloved relatives!

No near and dear, no kith, no kin. Everyone was over the previous night. Dinner at the table with the leaves and the good plates. Viands piled high, wine by the jerobaum, pies galore, coffee whose stimulative properties were sufficient to get everyone up and over to the door, where the women stood and talked in their coats for half an hour while the men jangled their keys. You bade them good-bye and walked back to turn off the lights in the little miniature village you set up every year. It's all done.

But hold on. What's the standard Christmas image? Babe, manger, goat, parents, the Orient Kings, and a dark night outside the rude barn. In other words, you realized, that's about *now*. When you think about it, Jesus appears to have been born around 10:00 p.m. on Christmas night—the point at which you had had enough Christmas, thank you very much.

Makes you think of the revelation you had a few years ago when the Cherub Choir at church sang the Norwegian classic, "I Am So Glad Each Christmas Eve." Or "I Yam So Gled," as the old men with white whiskers said it. The lyrics:

> I am so glad each Christmas Eve,
> the night of Jesus' birth!
> Then like the sun the Star shone forth,
> and angels sang on earth.

You realized that your entire life you'd been singing this song without realizing that Christmas Eve cannot be the night of

Jesus' birth. So maybe *this* is Christmas, right here. Everything's done—church, Santa, presents, family. But this *is* it, right here. The moment. The thing it's all about. Or not: Your Orthodox friends won't be getting around to this for two more weeks. Some say it happened in the spring. Well, as the Man said, you shall know not the day or the time.

Never mind. It's done, that's what matters.

It wasn't always so. You remember the Miracle of the Replenished Stocking. Back when I believed in Santa, I found something in my stocking the morning of the twenty-sixth. Don't recall what prompted me to palpate the sock for additional booty, but there was something in the toe, a small box. I pulled it out and discovered . . . a new needle for my 45 RPM monaural Woolworth tune box. Santa knew! He knew I'd been playing records with the equivalent of a roofing nail, and could now listen to the brilliant range of sounds from my *Flipper* theme song 45. (I played it over and over until my father accidentally stepped on it. I think I was fifty years old with my own child before I realized it had been a premeditated act.) For a few years after, I checked the stocking on the morning of the twenty-sixth, just to see if there was something. You could say I was trying to keep the spirit of Christmas alive beyond the standard parameters. You could say I was just a greedy little cuss. Eventually I stopped looking, because the twenty-sixth now meant something else: *Spend that double-sawbuck the grandparents slipped you.*

Off to Northport Shopping Center, a half block from my Fargo home. It had a drugstore with comic books and a squeaky rack filled with sci-fi paperbacks, a Ben Franklin with records and turtles and Revell models of Irwin Allen spaceships you could glue together and put on your shelf. All the decorations were still out; everything still felt like Christmas, but it was freed of all the solemn, long-face, good-hearted God stuff that you always felt obliged to observe during the run-up.

At least in front of the grown-ups. But there were always grown-ups around, even when there weren't.

The day after was a fine day in its own way, but by the evening there was a sad ache to it all. The tree was empty. The box of Russell Stover chocolates was picked over, with nothing but those dreadful squares filled with a thick cherry slurry. The presents had been integrated in your life, their novelty diminished by a few degrees. Suddenly you missed the anticipation. You remembered driving back from church through the darkened city, everything closed, knowing that Swedish meatballs and presents were next. It didn't get any better than that, and now you were on the other side of it with just $3.67 left from the grandparents' moneybomb.

Grim. But that was childhood. Now you're an adult, and when you wake on December 26th you're happy to go back to work. The idea of sitting in a cube looking at email actually has a certain appeal, the way a broke and hungover Roman galley rower might be relieved to shackle himself to the bench after a long, wild liberty. A man can only take so much happiness. So you get up and shower and listen to the radio. Dire traffic around the mall. All those kids cashing in their cards; bargain hunters snatching up discounted ornaments for next year's tree. SWEATER PRICES HAVE NEVER BEEN THIS LOW.

They wouldn't catch you dead in that madhouse. That's where your daughter will go, of course. She's got a couple of grandparent Franklins eager to be busted up and frittered away.

On the way out of the house to the office, you see the tree. You nod: *I understand this must be confusing for you.* Could be worse, bud: Some people take down the tree the next day, as if it's a sponging relative who had until the twenty-sixth to find a job and move out. There's something almost shocking about seeing the corpse on the boulevard; you almost imagine the family sitting around with stopwatches the previous night, waiting for the second hand to sweep past twelve. ALL RIGHT, SEASON OF JOY NOW CONCLUDED. COMMENCE DISASSEMBLY! HUT! HUT! HUT!

If you could ask the trees on the boulevard how they feel about this, you'd get no reply. Because of course they are cylinders of nonsentient cellulose, but also because it would be too humiliating for the tree to admit what it thought the day you brought it home. Pride of place. Bedecked with orbs of delicate glass. The shining faces of children as they hung small objects on you in veneration. The late nights when the Lady and the Man would sit on the sofa and gaze at the tree, talking about Christmases past. Of course it was all an elaborate ceremony, like putting the feathers of a rare bird around the neck of a man before he's led to the pyramid and has his heart carved out. The Man swore as he took you down to the boulevard. He actually did that dusting-off-his-hands thing. *Hope you got sap on your pants, fella. Hope you got some needles down your shirt.*

The other trees on the boulevard wouldn't say anything. They'd seen this before. They saw it every year. No point in warning them. I mean, if the fact that the house has a *floor made of trees* didn't tell you this wasn't any fancy, holy, tree place, nothing would. Maybe the logs in the fire might have been a clue, too.

But our tree is artificial, so it doesn't go out on the boulevard. I yank it apart into three segments, each of which has floppy metal limbs that hang out like busted bird wings. It came "pre-lit," like a relative who shows up for the party already half-drunk, so you have to sever the tendons of the lighting cord after you've separated the spine. I wrap it in a shroud and put it on a shelf in the garage; now and then a limb will flop out from under the sheets like the hand on a plague wagon headed for the dump.

My dad also has an artificial one. He doesn't take the decorations off, because he's eighty-nine and to heck with that. Down it goes in the basement, all its ornaments still attached. This seems wrong. The joy of the season is putting up the decorations, telling their stories, remembering where you got them. The finality of the season is plain when everything goes back in the box, when the lid closes over Mickey Mouse's grin. When the Nutcracker soldier is teeth-side down under a bristling thicket of ornament hangers. When you get everything back into the red bins, drag them downstairs, and store them in the back room in their accustomed place. You think,

Next time I see those it'll seem like yesterday. As if the year flared like a struck match and guttered out halfway down the stick. How old was Andrew Marvell when he talked about time's wingèd chariot? Thirty? Brother, you've no idea. Wait until you look at the calendar and your face ripples from G-forces because the chariot got a nitro-burning turbocharger.

⚜

"So did you put up the tree?" I asked Dad last year. That was a few months after his wife died. He hadn't brought up the tree. It spent the season with the furnace for company. I don't expect it to come up this year either. It would remind him that it hadn't been up last year, and why. Maybe next year.

Maybe never. It's not that he's anti-holiday. You'll find him in the pews every Sunday and twice on Christmas, mumbling "I Yam So Gled" with the rest of the congregation. But the end of Christmas always seemed to make him sad in a way that unnerves a kid, makes you think that there are vast private provinces of adult emotions you can never see until you find yourself there some day, squinting at the horizon, wishing you had a map. The AM radio on the kitchen counter always played carols, of course—standards old and new, pious and secular— and in the waning hours of Christmas Day, Dad would listen, noting how this was his favorite music. "I wish they'd play it all year," he said once. But when December 26 came around the tremulous melodies were shelved and it was Buck Owens again, buckaroos. Even Santa must get tired of that jingle-jingle stuff. You imagine Santa gets up on the twenty-sixth and it's all Led Zeppelin or doo-wop.

My father was Santa, by the way. I don't just mean he was the guy who filled the stockings after the kids were to bed. When he opened his Texaco station on the far, far end of town in December of '62 he had a grand opening, complete with Santa. Mom brought me out to the station to sit in the merry old man's lap and tell him what I wanted. There was something familiar about this Santa, unlike the department store manqués or ho-ho TV bluffers. Something paternal and knowing. I don't know if I caught the twin hints—the Old Spice and the smell of Super Chief gas—but Santa seemed a lot like Dad, and sitting on his lap in the office they were one and the same. On Christmas I must have thought it really had been Santa, because I got everything I asked him for. But the same would go for Dad.

The day after Christmas in Fargo, the LPs that had been piled on top of the old RCA record player went back in the slot for another year. These days I clear them out of the iTunes library. Same records, too: the great Goodyear records from the early '60s, when it made perfect sense that tire companies would issue compilations of religious music. Firestone had a rival series, but we went with Goodyear. It isn't Christmas until the Andre Kostelanetz version of "We Three Kings" is played at plaster-cracking levels. But the day after? Playlist > Delete.

All but one song. I leave "In the Bleak Midwinter," scored

for small humble instruments, played with deliberate care like someone stepping out on ice he trusts will bear his weight, but knows care must still be taken. Midwinter? We should be so lucky. It's just begun, really. Bleak? The day after Christmas is a riot of bright activity. Daughter goes off to the mall with friends; people go back to work; the holiday spirit maintains, but seems freed of obligations. It's like a dance after a long wedding ceremony. At the end of the week waits New Year's Eve to scour every aspect of the sacred from the season and celebrate the click of the odometer turning over. I never understood this holiday. Nothing changes. Rent is due. The second of January is like finding yourself on the cold steps outside your house. Your coat is thin. The door behind you is locked. You're not sure if you have your keys. But there is hope:

> In the bleak midwinter, frosty wind made moan,
> earth stood hard as iron, water like a stone;
> snow had fallen, snow on snow, snow on snow,
> in the bleak midwinter, long ago.

> Our God, heaven cannot hold Him, nor earth sustain;
> heaven and earth shall flee away when He comes to
>   reign.
> In the bleak midwinter a stable place sufficed
> the Lord God Almighty, Jesus Christ.

Snow had fallen, snow on snow, snow on snow: no better description of January in these parts. No better way to sum up the weight you bear as the years gather. It's hard not to feel as though the year ahead is a task to complete, a sentence to serve, a wheel to turn. The axle creaks a bit more. The road's rut seems slightly deeper. Good Lord, wasn't it just January 2 the other day?

No. No, it was not. It was 365 days ago, and while the return of

Christmas will bring you up short, convinced you just entombed the Mickey Mouse ornament a month ago, every day was a full sentence, every week a story, every month a thick book. Every year a new row on the shelf.

Yes, it starts and ends here, in the cold, in the snow, in the world of white fields and bare trees. But in the middle came the great green glory. It's what you remember when all is cold; it's what you assume to be the natural state of the world when the leaves and flowers rule. It's the loss you lament in the sumptuous swoon of autumn. Winter is the bill for the seasons that came before, but like all the other debts you piled up over Christmas, you'll pay it.

You're never so broke as you are on December 26th. And you're never so rich.

About the Contributors

CHRISTOPHER BUCKLEY is the author of seventeen books, including his latest novel, *The Relic Master*, a comic adventure set in sixteenth-century Europe. His previous books include *Thank You for Smoking*, made into a successful movie in 2005, and his acclaimed memoir, *Losing Mum and Pup*. His essays and journalism have been widely published. His awards include the Thurber Prize for American Humor and the Washington Irving Medal for Literary Excellence.

SONNY BUNCH is the executive editor of, and film critic for, the *Washington Free Beacon*. Previously he worked as a film critic for the *Washington Times* and has written about films and the film industry for the *Wall Street Journal*, the *Washington Post*, the *Weekly Standard*, and elsewhere. He lives in Alexandria, Virginia, with his wife and daughter.

DAVID "IOWAHAWK" Burge has successfully reproduced twice, resulting in a daughter (twenty-two) and a son (nineteen) far better than he deserves. He is also the proprietor of Iowahawk (iowahawk.typepad.com), considered by some to be one of the best sites on the Internet. His writing has also appeared in the *Weekly Standard*, *Big Hollywood*, *Garage Magazine*, *The Seven Deadly Virtues*, and *The Dadly Virtues*. He lives in Austin, Texas.

CHRISTOPHER CALDWELL is a senior editor at the *Weekly Standard* and the author of *Reflections on the Revolution in Europe* (Doubleday/Penguin). His essays and reviews appear in many U.S. and European publications.

JOSEPH EPSTEIN has two books forthcoming: *Wind Sprints: Shorter Essays* (Axios Press) and *Frozen in Time: Twenty Stories* (Rowman and Littlefield).

ANDREW FERGUSON is a senior editor at the *Weekly Standard* and the author most recently of *Crazy U: One Dad's Crash Course in Getting His Kid into College.*

JONAH GOLDBERG is a senior editor of *National Review* and a fellow at the American Enterprise Institute. A Fox News contributor, he is the author of two *New York Times* best sellers, *Liberal Fascism* and *The Tyranny of Clichés.* He is currently working on a new book in which his dog, Zoë, has absolutely no interest.

MICHAEL GRAHAM is a writer and radio talk-show host living in Atlanta, Georgia.

STEPHEN F. HAYES is a senior writer at the *Weekly Standard* and a Fox News contributor.

MOLLIE HEMINGWAY is senior editor at the *Federalist,* a web magazine focused on culture, politics, and religion. A longtime journalist, her writing on religion, economics, and baseball has appeared in the *Wall Street Journal,* the *Los Angeles Times,* the *Guardian, Federal Times, Radio & Records,* and *Modern Reformation.* Originally from Colorado, she lives in northern Virginia with her husband and two children. She enjoys combing flea markets to improve her vinyl record collection and believes that the designated hitter rule is the result of a communist plot.

She is a regular commentator on both television and radio and has appeared on outlets ranging from CNN and the BBC to Fox News Channel and NPR.

MATT LABASH is a senior writer at the *Weekly Standard*. His collection *Fly-Fishing with Darth Vader: And Other Adventures with Evangelical Wrestlers, Political Hitmen, and Jewish Cowboys* was published in 2010 by Simon and Schuster. He lives in Owings, Maryland.

JONATHAN V. LAST is a senior writer at the *Weekly Standard* and editor of *The Seven Deadly Virtues* and *The Dadly Virtues*. In 2013 he published *What to Expect When No One's Expecting: America's Coming Demographic Disaster,* which is probably the funniest book ever written about demographics. He lives in Virginia with his wife and three children, the youngest of whom was born two days after Christmas. She dodged a bullet.

JAMES LILEKS is a Metro columnist, blogger, and video producer for the *Star Tribune* in Minneapolis. He writes the *Athwart!* column in *National Review* and appears fortnightly on *National Review Online*. Full responsibility for the inordinately large pop-culture repository of lileks.com is his, and he writes *The Bleat* Monday to Friday at that very address. *The Casablanca Tango*, his latest, a newspaper-noir novel, can be found on Amazon.com. He hates biographical paragraphs that end with some small, winsome detail, like this one.

ROB LONG is a writer and producer in Hollywood. He began his career writing and producing TV's long-running *Cheers*, and served as coexecutive producer in its final season. During his time on the series, *Cheers* received two Emmy Awards and two Golden Globe Awards. Long has been nominated twice for an Emmy Award, and has received a Writers Guild of

America Award. He continues to work in film and television in Los Angeles. His two books, *Conversations with My Agent* and *Set Up, Joke, Set Up, Joke*, were republished as a set in 2014 by Bloomsbury. Long is a contributing editor to *National Review* and a weekly columnist for the *National*, Abu Dhabi's English-language daily newspaper. His weekly radio commentary, *Martini Shot*, is broadcast on the Los Angeles public radio station KCRW and is distributed nationally as a podcast. He is a cofounder of the fast-growing Ricochet.com, the place for smart and stimulating conversation—on the Web and mobile devices—from a center/right perspective.

LARRY MILLER is an actor, comedian, voice artist, podcaster, and columnist. He has appeared in over one hundred films and television shows, including *Seinfeld* and *10 Things I Hate about You*, as well as several characters in Christopher Guest's mockumentary films. His other credits include *Pretty Woman*, *The Nutty Professor*, *Nutty Professor II: The Klumps*, *Law & Order*, and *Boston Legal*. In addition, he's a contributing humorist to the *Huffington Post* and the *Weekly Standard*, as well as the author of the best-selling book *Spoiled Rotten America*. Miller hosts the podcast *The Larry Miller Show*, where he unleashes a barrage of humor about the absurdities of daily life.

P. J. O'ROURKE's new book is *Thrown under the Omnibus*, an anthology of forty years of his work, if that's the word. Buy it for the Patrick Oliphant cover art.

KIRSTEN POWERS is a columnist for *USA Today*, a Fox News contributor, and the *New York Times* best-selling author of *The Silencing: How the Left Is Killing Free Speech*. Prior to her career in journalism, Powers was a political appointee in the Clinton administration from 1993 to 1998 where she served as deputy assistant U.S. trade representative for public affairs. She later worked in New York State and City Democratic politics, including serving as press secretary for Andrew Cuomo's 2002 governor's race and as a consultant to the New York State Democratic Committee. Her writing has been published in the *Wall Street Journal*, *USA Today*, the *Dallas Morning News*, the *New York Observer*, *Salon.com*, the *Daily Beast*, the *New York Post*, *Elle* magazine, and *American Prospect* online. A native of Fairbanks, Alaska, Powers currently resides in Washington, D.C.

JOE QUEENAN writes the *Moving Targets* column for the *Wall Street Journal*. Author of nine books, he is a graduate of St. Joseph's College in Philadelphia. He has two children: a lawyer and a doctor of neuroscience.

HEATHER WILHELM is a weekly columnist for RealClearPolitics and a senior contributor at the *Federalist*. Her syndicated column appears in the *Chicago Tribune*, the *Dallas Morning News*, and other outlets nationwide. Her work has also appeared in *Commentary*, the *Wall Street Journal*, the *Washington Examiner*, and *National Review Online*. A former Chicagoan, Heather is now a fully converted and enthusiastic Texan, and as you know, the converts are the worst. She lives in Austin, Texas with her husband and three children.

TOBY YOUNG has worked as a feature writer, a film critic, a political columnist, and a judge on *Top Chef* over the course of his thirty-year career as a journalist. He is the author of *How to Lose Friends and Alienate People*, a memoir about his adventures at *Vanity Fair* magazine in New York, and coproduced the film of the same name. He is currently an associate editor of the *Spectator*, where he has written a weekly column since 1998.